Children's Illustrated
HISTORY ATLAS

Authors Simon Adams, Peter Chrisp
Senior editor Lizzie Davey
Project art editor Hoa Luc

Map illustrator Jeongeun Park
Cartography Ed Merritt
Illustrator Molly Lattin
Editorial Abhijit Dutta, Satu Fox,
Roohi Sehgal, Kathleen Teece, Amina Youssef
Design Yamini Panwar, Nehal Verma
US Senior editor Shannon Beatty
US Editor Liz Searcy
Picture researcher Sumita Khatwani
Jacket coordinator Francesca Young
Jacket designer Suzena Sengupta
Managing editor Laura Gilbert
Managing art editor Diane Peyton Jones
Pre-production producer Dragana Puvacic
Producer Basia Ossowska
Design director Helen Senior
Publishing director Sarah Larter

First American Edition, 2018
Published in the United States by DK Publishing
345 Hudson Street, New York, New York 10014

Copyright © 2018 Dorling Kindersley Limited
DK, a Division of Penguin Random House LLC
18 19 20 21 22 10 9 8 7 6 5 4 3 2 1
001-308500-Aug/2018

A catalog record for this book is available from the Library of Congress.

DK books are available at special discounts when purchased in bulk for sales promotions, premiums, fund-raising, or educational use. For details, contact: DK Publishing Special Markets, 345 Hudson Street, New York, New York 10014 SpecialSales@dk.com

ISBN: 978-1-4654-7031-7

Printed and bound in Malaysia.

A WORLD OF IDEAS:
SEE ALL THERE IS TO KNOW
www.dk.com

Contents

⚙ Smithsonian

This trademark is owned by the Smithsonian Institution and is registered
in the U.S Patent and Trademark Office.

Consultant Dr. F. Robert van der Linden, Curator of Air Transportation and
Special Purpose Aircraft, Smithsonian's National Air and Space Museum

Smithsonian Enterprises
Product Development Manager
Kealy Gordon
Licensing Manager
Ellen Nanney
Vice President, Consumer and Education Products
Brigid Ferraro
Senior Vice President, Consumer and Education Products
Carol LeBlanc

Established in 1846, the Smithsonian Institution—the world's largest
museum and research complex—includes 19 museums and galleries
and the National Zoological Park. The total number of objects, works
of art, and specimens in the Smithsonian's collection is estimated
at 154 million. The Smithsonian is a renowned research center,
dedicated to public education, national service, and scholarship in
the arts, sciences, and history.

How to use this book

A map is a drawing that gives an overall view of a place. The maps in this book show parts of the world at different times in history. The countries and territories these maps show often look very different from how these same places appear today.

Outside areas
Around the edges of many of the maps are other land areas. These are shown in a cream color.

Dates
On the map, dates are shown in bold, to help you find your way around the page.

Picture features
Pictures with text highlight special features, including buildings and battles.

Important cities
Capital cities are marked with red outlines. Other cities are outlined in blue.

Ancient Rome

More than 2,000 years ago, ancient Rome was one of the most powerful nations in the world. At first, Rome was ruled by kings. It became a republic in 509 BCE, which meant that it was ruled by members of Roman society. In 27 BCE Rome became an empire, led by a ruler called an emperor. At its largest, in 117 CE, the Roman Empire was home to more than 65 million people.

Named after Emperor Hadrian, work on this wall began in 122 CE. It marked the northwest edge of the empire.

Hadrian's Wall

NORTH SEA

The Appian Way leading

Snapshots
These images add extra information about historical events, people, and places.

Punic Wars
Between 264 and 146 BCE, Rome fought three wars against the city of Carthage, in modern-day Tunisia. Rome wanted control of the Mediterranean Sea. The wars, known as the Punic Wars, ended in total Roman victory.

This leader of the Arverni tribe led an uprising against Roman power in 52 BCE.

The Romans built this lighthouse in what is now Spain.

This was the most important gold mine in the Roman Empire.

Vercingetorix

Roman roads
The Romans built many lon link the towns and cities of paved roads helped soldiers around the empire

Pont du Gard

Tower of Hercules

Las Medulas

Verona Arena

Key
The key gives information about the picture symbols on the map.

General Hannibal from Carthage

KEY (c.117 CE)

Empire border	The edge of the Roman Empire.
Grain	Shipped to Rome from North Africa and Sicily.
Grapevines	Vines were planted across the empire to grow grapes to make into wine.
Timber	Forests were stripped of wood all over the empire.
Roman baths	Public bathing brought the Romans together.
Slaves	Many Romans owned slaves. Some slaves had to build Roman roads.
Amphitheaters	Open-air theaters entertained Romans across the empire.
Roman soldiers	The army kept the peace and defended the borders against enemy invasion.

Date
Some of the keys have a date to show the time period of the map. If the date includes "c.," it means "circa," or "around"—meaning the date isn't exact.

The Romans built aqueducts to transport water from one place to another.

Rome

Mount Vesuvius

The city o was destr the erupti volcano N Vesuvius i

ATLANTIC OCEAN

MEDITERRANEAN SEA

Carthaginians

Theater at Djemila

The Romans built this amphitheater in what is now Tunisia.

The Carthaginians used war elephants to fight against the Roman Empire.

Julius Caesar
One of ancient Rome's most well-known leaders, Julius Caesar conquered large amounts of land for Rome. The empire began with his great-nephew, Augustus, who made himself the first emperor.

An important city in Roman Libya.

Leptis Magna

SCALE

0   200 miles

0   200 kilometers

Compass
The compass always points to north (N) on the map and also shows the direction of south (S), east (E), and west (W).

Picture symbols
You will find picture symbols without text on some of the maps. Look at the key to find out what each symbol means.

Scale
The scale indicates the size of the country and the distances between different points on the map.

States at war

The five kingdoms each battled to become the most powerful. They were eventually united into the huge empire of China.

These mini-maps show you where an area is in the world.

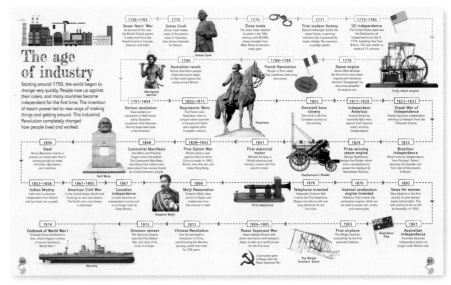

The age of industry

Starting around 1750, the world began to change very quickly. People rose up against their rulers, and many countries became independent for the first time. The invention of steam power led to new ways of making things and getting around. This Industrial Revolution completely changed how people lived and worked.

Timelines

Each chapter starts with a timeline spread. The timelines show you events in different parts of the world in the order that they happened.

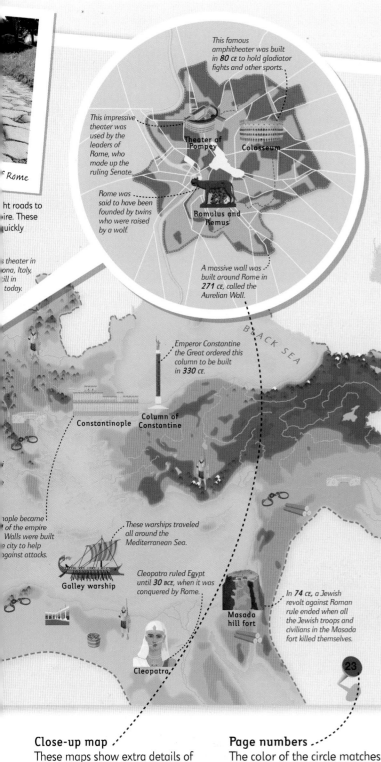

This famous amphitheater was built in **80** CE to hold gladiator fights and other sports.

This impressive theater was used by the leaders of Rome, who made up the ruling Senate.

Theater of Pompey

Colosseum

Rome was said to have been founded by twins who were raised by a wolf.

Romulus and Remus

A massive wall was built around Rome in **271** CE, called the Aurelian Wall.

BLACK SEA

Emperor Constantine the Great ordered this column to be built in **330** CE.

Constantinople

Column of Constantine

...ople became ...of the empire ...Walls were built ...city to help ...against attacks.

These warships traveled all around the Mediterranean Sea.

Galley warship

Cleopatra ruled Egypt until **30** BCE, when it was conquered by Rome.

Masada hill fort

In **74** CE, a Jewish revolt against Roman rule ended when all the Jewish troops and civilians in the Masada fort killed themselves.

Cleopatra

23

Close-up map
These maps show extra details of interesting areas that would be too small to show on the main maps.

Page numbers
The color of the circle matches the chapter color and tells you which chapter you are in.

How years are numbered

Each year is given a number to help people keep track of what happened (and happens) when. These numbers are called dates. Here are some things that are useful to know about historical dates.

CE and BCE

You will see that some dates have "CE" or "BCE" after them. CE means "Common Era" and BCE means "Before the Common Era." CE is used for dates after the year 1 BCE, and BCE for dates before 1 CE. In this book, if a date doesn't have CE or BCE after it, it is CE.

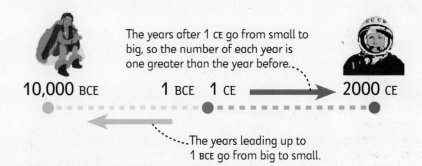

The years after 1 CE go from small to big, so the number of each year is one greater than the year before.

10,000 BCE   1 BCE   1 CE   2000 CE

The years leading up to 1 BCE go from big to small.

Centuries

A century is a period of 100 years. Historians often talk about periods of time using centuries, for example, "the 18th century." The years covered by a century are the 100 leading up to it. So the 18th century covers the years 1700–1799. Here are some examples.

Century	Time covered	Century	Time covered
14th century	1300–1399 CE	18th century	1700–1799 CE
15th century	1400–1499 CE	19th century	1800–1899 CE
16th century	1500–1599 CE	20th century	1900–1999 CE
17th century	1600–1699 CE	21st century	2000–2099 CE

World people

The human story began in Africa six million years ago, when apes began to walk upright on two legs. Over time, humanlike apes, called hominins, grew bigger and more intelligent. Our species, *Homo sapiens*, appeared in Africa 200,000 years ago. Around 120,000 years ago, some of them left Africa to spread all over the world.

Fire maker

Homo erectus (upright man) was the first hominin to leave Africa, 1.8 million years ago. They were the same height as we are, but their faces were more apelike. They made stone axes and learned to control fire.

Homo erectus

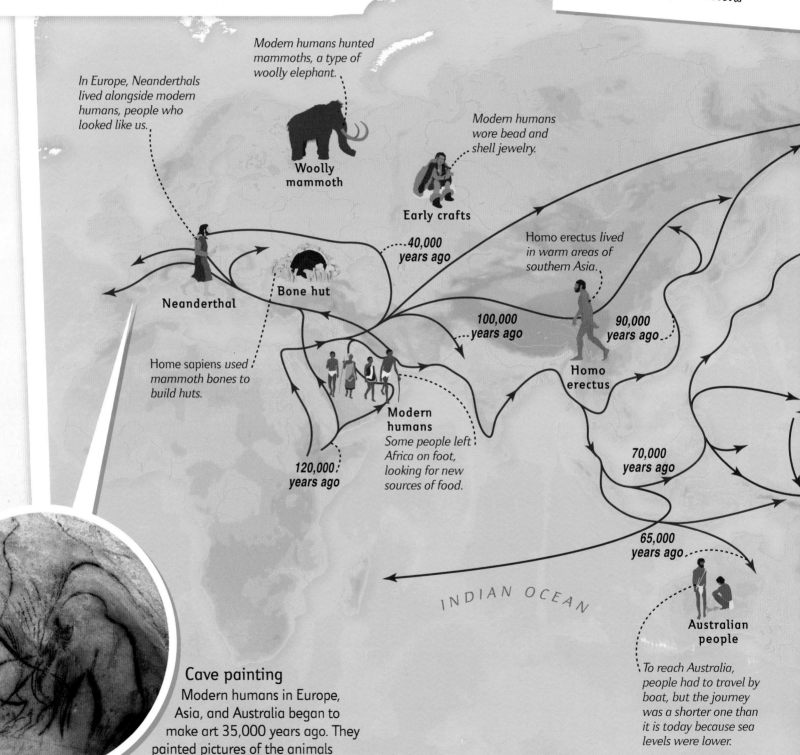

In Europe, Neanderthals lived alongside modern humans, people who looked like us.

Modern humans hunted mammoths, a type of woolly elephant.

Modern humans wore bead and shell jewelry.

Woolly mammoth

Early crafts

40,000 years ago

Homo erectus *lived in warm areas of southern Asia.*

Neanderthal

Bone hut

100,000 years ago

90,000 years ago

Home sapiens *used mammoth bones to build huts.*

Homo erectus

Modern humans
Some people left Africa on foot, looking for new sources of food.

120,000 years ago

70,000 years ago

INDIAN OCEAN

65,000 years ago

Australian people

To reach Australia, people had to travel by boat, but the journey was a shorter one than it is today because sea levels were lower.

Cave painting
Modern humans in Europe, Asia, and Australia began to make art 35,000 years ago. They painted pictures of the animals they hunted on the walls of caves.

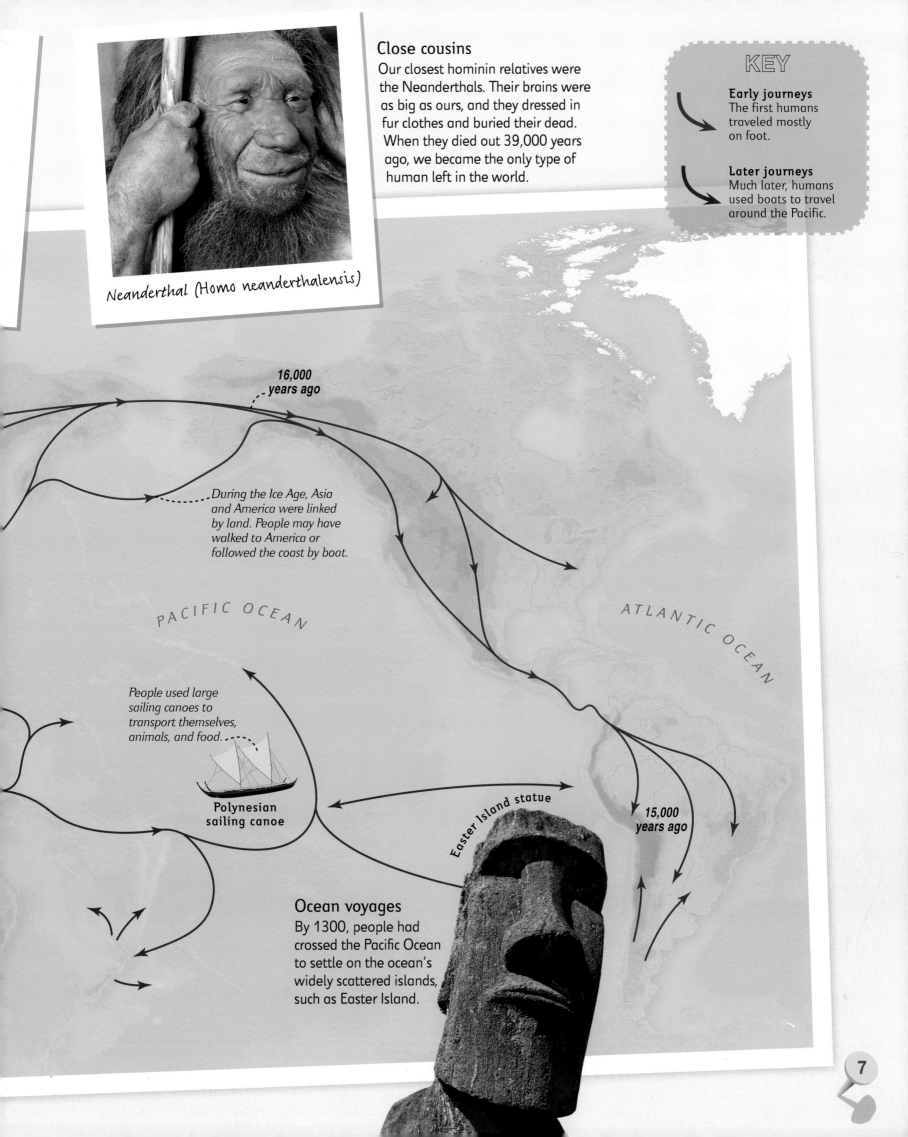

Close cousins

Our closest hominin relatives were the Neanderthals. Their brains were as big as ours, and they dressed in fur clothes and buried their dead. When they died out 39,000 years ago, we became the only type of human left in the world.

Neanderthal (Homo neanderthalensis)

16,000 years ago

During the Ice Age, Asia and America were linked by land. People may have walked to America or followed the coast by boat.

PACIFIC OCEAN

ATLANTIC OCEAN

People used large sailing canoes to transport themselves, animals, and food.

Polynesian sailing canoe

Easter Island statue

15,000 years ago

Ocean voyages

By 1300, people had crossed the Pacific Ocean to settle on the ocean's widely scattered islands, such as Easter Island.

7

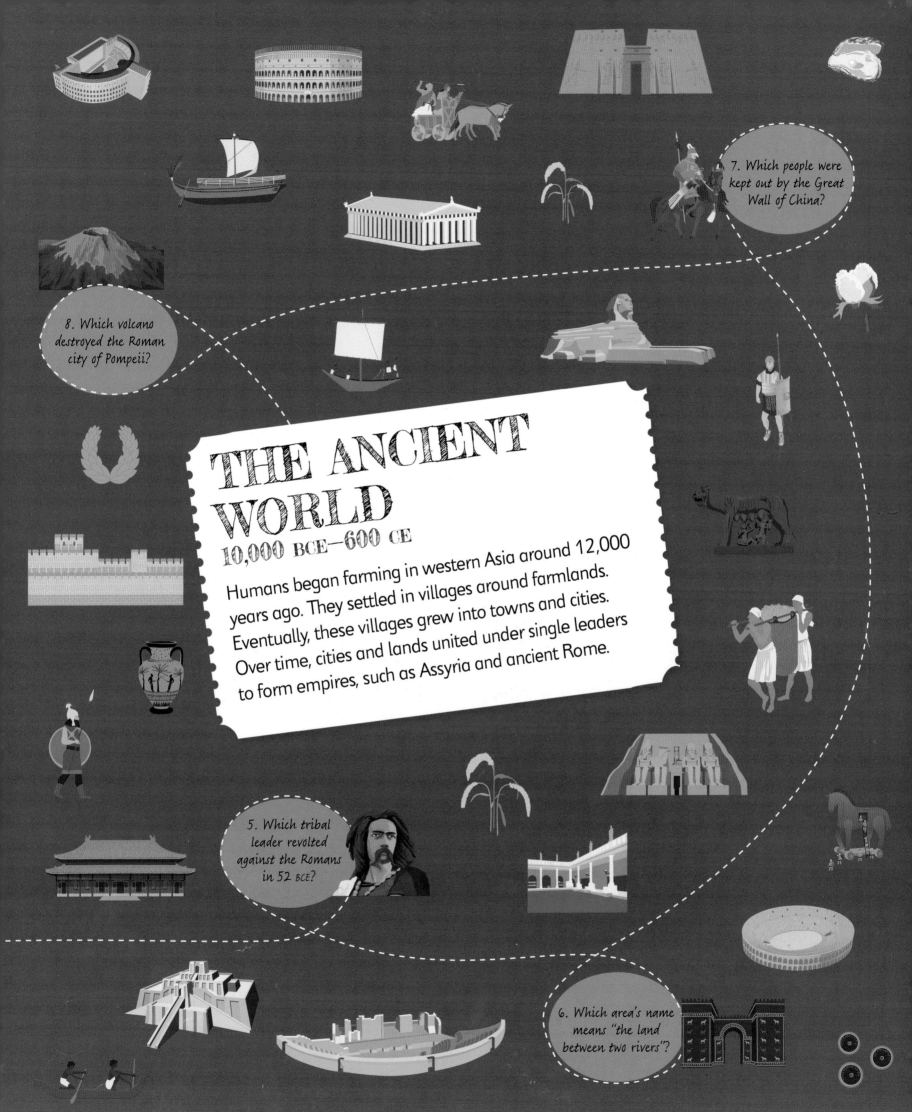

THE ANCIENT WORLD
10,000 BCE–600 CE

Humans began farming in western Asia around 12,000 years ago. They settled in villages around farmlands. Eventually, these villages grew into towns and cities. Over time, cities and lands united under single leaders to form empires, such as Assyria and ancient Rome.

7. Which people were kept out by the Great Wall of China?

8. Which volcano destroyed the Roman city of Pompeii?

5. Which tribal leader revolted against the Romans in 52 BCE?

6. Which area's name means "the land between two rivers"?

The ancient world

For most of the past, people lived as hunter-gatherers. They moved around, hunted animals, and gathered wild plants. After the last Ice Age—a long period of cold weather—ended about 11,500 years ago, people learned how to farm. Planting crops and raising animals meant people had to settle down in one place. The number of people grew, and villages became towns. Soon states and empires were also created.

35,000 years ago
First art
People in Europe and Asia make the first works of art—cave paintings and carvings of animals and people.

5000 BCE
First metal tools
People in Europe and western Asia begin to make tools, such as axes, from copper instead of stone.

4000 BCE
World's first city
Villages at Uruk in Sumer (southern Iraq) join together to create the world's first city.

Bronze Age spear

2613–2503 BCE
Great Pyramids built
Egyptian pharaohs build huge pyramid tombs at Giza.

2500 BCE
Indus cities
The Indus, or Harappan, people build cities in the Indus Valley of northwest India. They also grow cotton for cloth.

Pyramids at Giza

2500 BCE
First recorded war
The first recorded war in history is fought, between the Sumerian cities of Lagash and Umma.

c.2300 BCE
First empire
King Sargon of Akkad conquers Mesopotamia and creates the world's first empire.

117 CE
Roman Empire
The Roman Empire reaches its largest size under Emperor Trajan. It stretches from Spain in the west to Iraq in the east.

221–210 CE
China's first emperor
China is united under the First Emperor. When he dies, he is buried in a tomb protected by a terra-cotta (clay) army.

Terra-cotta army

Woolly mammoth

14,000–9,000 years ago
The climate warms
The world gets warmer; sea levels rise; and forests spread. Many big animals, such as mammoths, die out.

Jomon pot

13,000 BCE
Pottery invented
The Jomon people of Japan make the world's oldest known pottery.

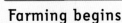

6500 BCE
Earliest silk making
Silk begins to be spun in China. Silk is a fine fabric made from the cocoons of the silk moth.

Silk worms

7000 BCE
First cloth woven
People in the Fertile Crescent learn to weave cloth from the fibers of a plant called flax.

10,000 BCE
Farming begins
In the Fertile Crescent, stretching from Egypt to Iraq, people begin to plant wheat and barley and raise animals for meat and milk.

3300 BCE
Writing invented
Egyptians invent the world's first writing system, hieroglyphs.

Egyptian hieroglyphs

3100 BCE
Egypt united
Egypt becomes a single kingdom under the rule of a pharaoh, perhaps called Narmer.

3000 BCE
Bronze Age begins
Mesopotamians mix tin and copper to make bronze, a harder metal. Soon after, bronze is also made in China.

3000 BCE
South American farming begins
Farming starts in the Andes mountains of South America, where people grow crops including potatoes.

South American potatoes

King Sargon

c.1200 BCE
Iron Age begins
The Bronze Age ends, and the Iron Age begins when people in Anatolia (modern Turkey) start making iron.

c.1200 BCE
First American civilizations
The Olmecs of Mesoamerica and the people of Chavin de Huantar in Peru live in the first American civilizations.

c.1000–500 BCE
Farming spreads in Africa
Farming people move from Nigeria to settle across much of Africa. They grow yams, millet, and sorghum. In 400 BCE, they begin making iron tools.

334–323 BCE
Alexander the Great
After uniting Greece, Alexander the Great of Macedonia conquers an empire stretching from Egypt to India.

c.500–336 BCE
Ancient Greece
Greek civilization is at its peak. The Greeks create beautiful art and architecture and invent science, philosophy, theater, history writing, and politics.

Stonehenge

Farming people worked together to create huge monuments called megaliths, meaning "great stones." Some were tombs to bury the dead. Others, such as Stonehenge in Britain, were places for religious ceremonies.

Settling down

Farming began in Asia and then moved into Europe. People settled down in different places and started a variety of cultures.

Orkney

NORTH SEA

Funnelbeaker

In Denmark and Sweden, people made pots with funnel-shaped tops, called funnelbeakers.

Newgrange

In 10,000 BCE, Britain was connected to Europe. Later, around 6500 BCE, rising sea levels flooded this area, cutting Britain off.

ATLANTIC SEA

In central Europe, people decorated pots by scratching lines in the clay.

Salisbury

Early trade

After people settled down as farmers, they began to make things to trade, such as pots. The most prized objects for trading were polished stone axes, which people started making around 4000 BCE. They were traded across long distances.

Carnac

Carnac stones

In southern Europe, people decorated pots with cockleshells. Cardium is the Latin name for a cockle.

Linear pottery

Cardium pottery

Polished flint axes

TYRRHENIAN SEA

The Stone Age

The earliest period of our history is called the Stone Age because people used tools made from stone. They hunted wild animals and gathered wild plants. Later, starting around 10,000 BCE, people in East Asia began to plant crops and keep animals. Farming then spread west across Europe.

SCALE

0   200 miles

0   200 kilometers

Malta

W E N S

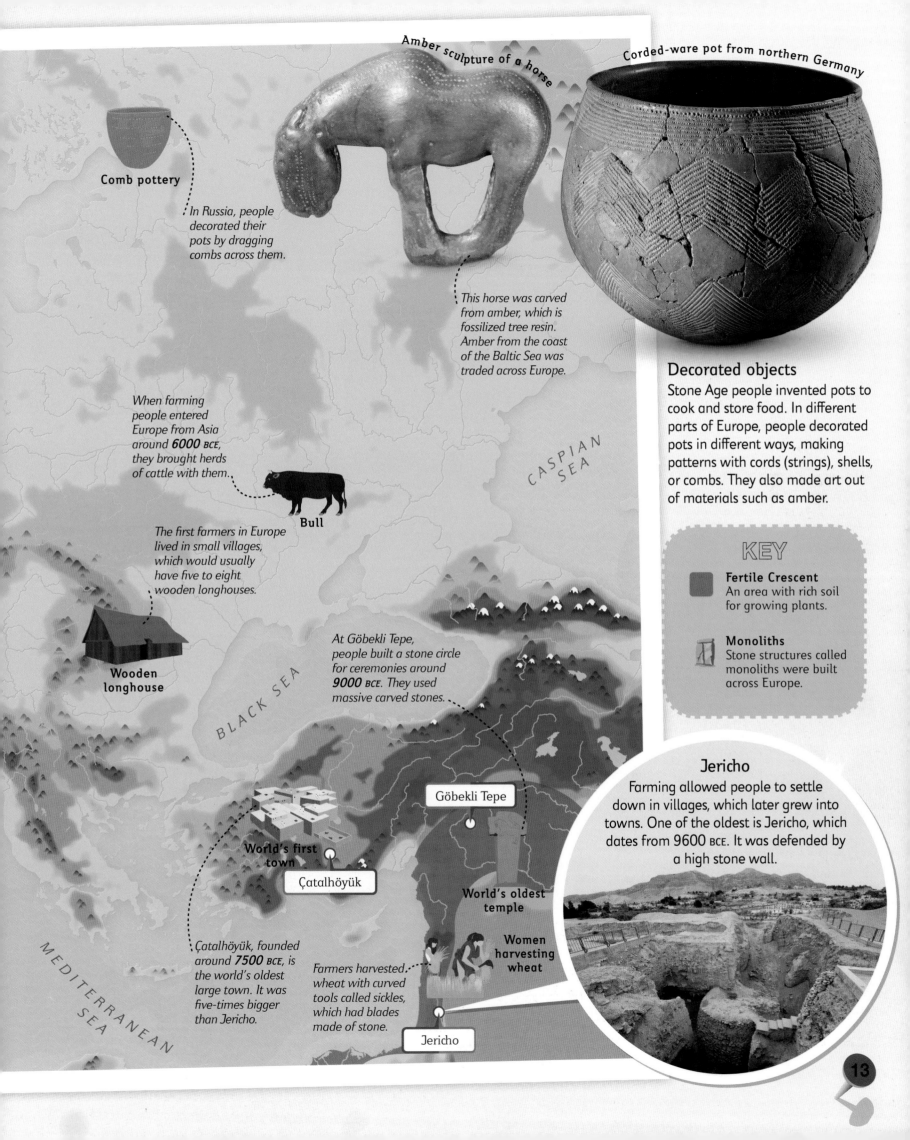

Comb pottery

Amber sculpture of a horse

Corded-ware pot from northern Germany

In Russia, people decorated their pots by dragging combs across them.

This horse was carved from amber, which is fossilized tree resin. Amber from the coast of the Baltic Sea was traded across Europe.

Decorated objects

Stone Age people invented pots to cook and store food. In different parts of Europe, people decorated pots in different ways, making patterns with cords (strings), shells, or combs. They also made art out of materials such as amber.

When farming people entered Europe from Asia around 6000 BCE, they brought herds of cattle with them.

CASPIAN SEA

Bull

The first farmers in Europe lived in small villages, which would usually have five to eight wooden longhouses.

KEY

Fertile Crescent
An area with rich soil for growing plants.

Monoliths
Stone structures called monoliths were built across Europe.

Wooden longhouse

At Göbekli Tepe, people built a stone circle for ceremonies around 9000 BCE. They used massive carved stones.

BLACK SEA

Göbekli Tepe

World's first town

Çatalhöyük

World's oldest temple

Women harvesting wheat

Jericho

Farming allowed people to settle down in villages, which later grew into towns. One of the oldest is Jericho, which dates from 9600 BCE. It was defended by a high stone wall.

Çatalhöyük, founded around 7500 BCE, is the world's oldest large town. It was five-times bigger than Jericho.

Farmers harvested wheat with curved tools called sickles, which had blades made of stone.

MEDITERRANEAN SEA

Jericho

Mesopotamia

Mesopotamia means "the land between the two rivers." It existed around the rivers Tigris and Euphrates in the Middle East. It was here, around 3300 BCE, that the world's first cities were built. Mesopotamian cities were ruled by kings, who waged war with each other using trained armies. The Mesopotamians invented bronze making and writing.

Writing

Mesopotamians invented one of the first writing systems. It is called cuneiform, which means "wedge shaped." It was written by pushing a sharp reed into a soft clay tablet. Cuneiform was used for 3,200 years across western Asia.

Cuneiform writing

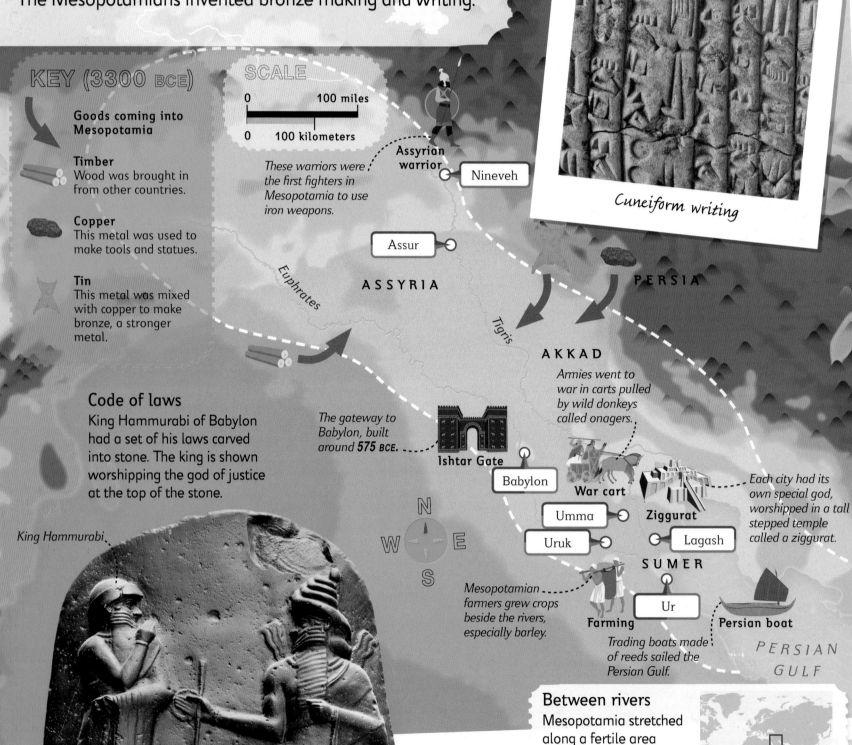

KEY (3300 BCE)

Goods coming into Mesopotamia

Timber
Wood was brought in from other countries.

Copper
This metal was used to make tools and statues.

Tin
This metal was mixed with copper to make bronze, a stronger metal.

SCALE

0 — 100 miles
0 — 100 kilometers

Assyrian warrior
These warriors were the first fighters in Mesopotamia to use iron weapons.

Nineveh

Assur

ASSYRIA

Euphrates

Tigris

PERSIA

AKKAD
Armies went to war in carts pulled by wild donkeys called onagers.

Code of laws

King Hammurabi of Babylon had a set of his laws carved into stone. The king is shown worshipping the god of justice at the top of the stone.

The gateway to Babylon, built around 575 BCE.

Ishtar Gate

Babylon

War cart

Ziggurat

Each city had its own special god, worshipped in a tall stepped temple called a ziggurat.

Umma

Uruk

Lagash

SUMER

Ur

King Hammurabi

N W E S

Mesopotamian farmers grew crops beside the rivers, especially barley.

Farming

Persian boat

Trading boats made of reeds sailed the Persian Gulf.

PERSIAN GULF

Shamash, god of justice

Between rivers

Mesopotamia stretched along a fertile area between the Tigris and Euphrates, which made it a good place to farm.

14

Indus Valley

The land around the Indus River was the birthplace of another of the first civilizations. Beginning around 2600 BCE, people here built carefully planned cities. This was the largest early civilization, bigger than Egypt and Mesopotamia put together. There is no evidence left of how the people of the Indus Valley were ruled.

Indus seal

The people of the Indus Valley invented a type of writing with around 300 picture signs, which we still cannot understand. It was used on carved stone seals, where the signs appeared above pictures of animals.

Ruins of Mohenjo-Daro

The biggest Indus city was Mohenjo-Daro. Every house had its own water supply, toilet, and bath.

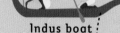

Indus boat

Harappa

Indus traders traveled by boat, taking goods along the rivers.

THAR DESERT

KEY (2600 BCE)

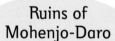

Goods coming into the Indus area

Silver
This metal was used to make jewelry.

Copper
This metal was used to make pots and knives.

Lapis lazuli
This blue stone from Afghanistan was used to make jewelry.

Tin
This metal was mixed with copper to make bronze.

Cotton growing
Cotton fibers were woven into cloth.

Carnelian

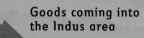

A red stone called carnelian was used to make beads for jewelry.

Mohenjo-Daro

Elephants were hunted for their ivory tusks.

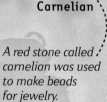

Asian elephant

Dholavira

Coastal people collected oysters to get the pearls sometimes found inside.

Pearls

Lothal

ARABIAN SEA

SCALE

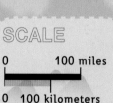

```
0          100 miles

0   100 kilometers
```

River network

The Indus civilization grew up around small rivers that flowed into the large Indus River, which ended at the Arabian Sea.

Ancient Egypt

Around 3000 BCE, the people who lived along the Nile River created one of the world's earliest civilizations, ancient Egypt. Kings known as pharaohs ruled Egypt for over 3,000 years. It was the most stable and longest-lasting civilization in the ancient world.

Hieroglyphs

The Egyptians invented hieroglyphs, the world's first writing system. Hieroglyphs were pictures that stood for things and ideas. They were carved in stone or written on a type of paper called papyrus.

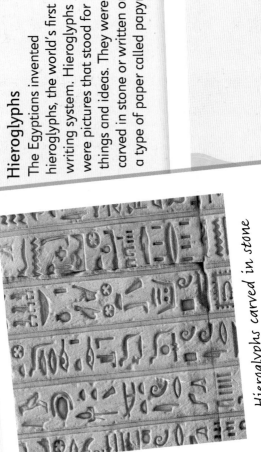

Hieroglyphs carved in stone

Fertile Nile

Egypt lies along the Nile River, which flows through the desert of northeast Africa into the Mediterranean Sea.

MEDITERRANEAN SEA

LOWER EGYPT

Memphis

Sphinx at Giza

Giza

The Sphinx, a statue of a lion with a human head, guards the pyramids.

Plowing

Farmers grew wheat and other crops next to the river.

Sailing south

Egyptian boats sailed south using the wind, which usually blows from north to south. The current carried them north again.

Pyramids of Giza

From 2650 to 1800 BCE, pharaohs were buried in huge stone tombs called pyramids. The Great Pyramid is the only survivor of the seven wonders of the ancient world.

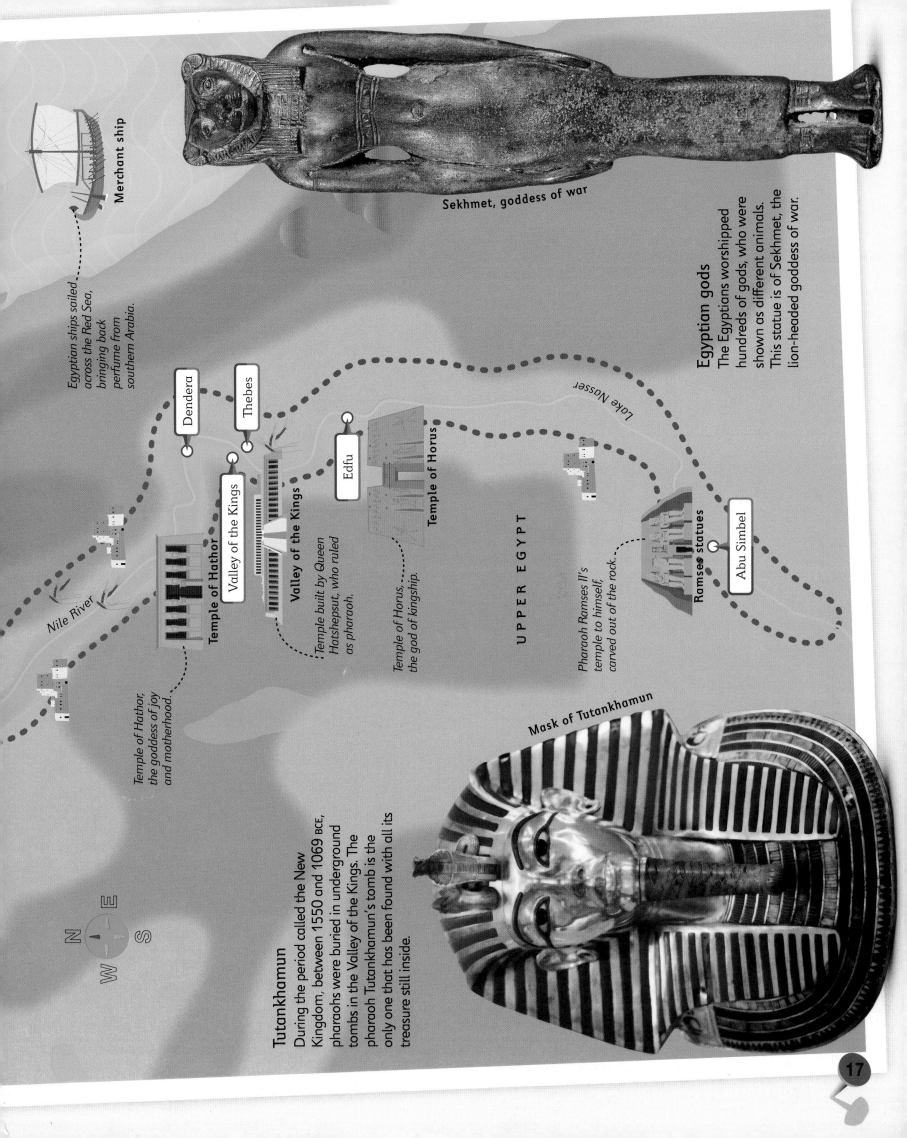

Merchant ship

Sekhmet, goddess of war

Egyptian ships sailed across the Red Sea, bringing back perfume from southern Arabia.

Egyptian gods
The Egyptians worshipped hundreds of gods, who were shown as different animals. This statue is of Sekhmet, the lion-headed goddess of war.

Dendera

Thebes

Edfu

Temple of Horus

Lake Nasser

Nile River

Temple of Hathor

Valley of the Kings

Temple of Hathor, the goddess of joy and motherhood.

Temple built by Queen Hatshepsut, who ruled as pharaoh.

Temple of Horus, the god of kingship.

U P P E R   E G Y P T

Ramses statues

Abu Simbel

Pharaoh Ramses II's temple to himself, carved out of the rock.

N
W   E
S

Tutankhamun
During the period called the New Kingdom, between 1550 and 1069 BCE, pharaohs were buried in underground tombs in the Valley of the Kings. The pharaoh Tutankhamun's tomb is the only one that has been found with all its treasure still inside.

Mask of Tutankhamun

KEY

 City-states
ATHENS Individual Greek cities ruled themselves and had their own armies.

 Merchant routes
Greek merchants sailed the seas, carrying goods such as olive oil.

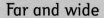 **Sea battles**
Warships were rowed into battle, using battering rams to sink enemy ships.

Greek games
Athletic contests were held in religious centers, such as Olympia.

Many cities
Ancient Greece was a collection of city-states. The Greeks traveled and founded cities all over the Mediterranean.

SCALE
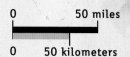
0   50 miles

0   50 kilometers

ADRIATIC SEA

 NAPLES

 PAESTUM

 SYRACUSE

IONIAN SEA

Far and wide
The Greeks founded settlements all around the Mediterranean and the Black Sea. The best surviving Greek temples are not in Greece but in Italy. This one is in Sicily.

Temple of Segesta, built c.420 BCE

The Olympic Games
The Greeks invented athletic competitions. The most famous was held at Olympia during a festival in honor of Zeus, king of the gods. Athletes came from all over the Greek world.

Ancient Greece

The ancient Greeks were some of the most creative people in history. They invented theater, sports, politics, science, and the writing of history. Their beautiful art and architecture is still copied today. Ancient Greek civilization was at its height between 500 and 300 BCE.

Wrestling in the Greek Olympics

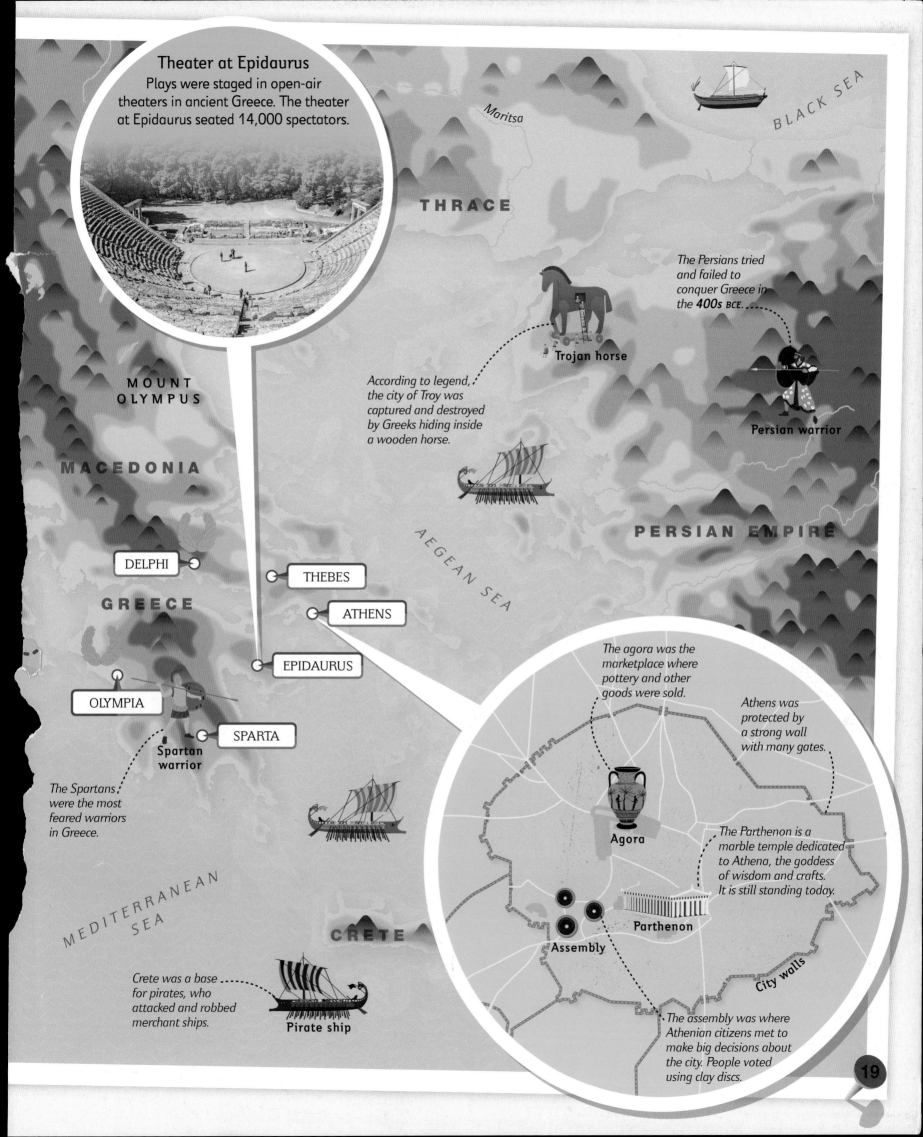

Theater at Epidaurus

Plays were staged in open-air theaters in ancient Greece. The theater at Epidaurus seated 14,000 spectators.

BLACK SEA

Maritsa

THRACE

The Persians tried and failed to conquer Greece in the **400s** BCE.

Trojan horse

According to legend, the city of Troy was captured and destroyed by Greeks hiding inside a wooden horse.

Persian warrior

MOUNT OLYMPUS

MACEDONIA

AEGEAN SEA

PERSIAN EMPIRE

DELPHI

GREECE

THEBES

ATHENS

EPIDAURUS

OLYMPIA

SPARTA

Spartan warrior

The Spartans were the most feared warriors in Greece.

The agora was the marketplace where pottery and other goods were sold.

Athens was protected by a strong wall with many gates.

Agora

The Parthenon is a marble temple dedicated to Athena, the goddess of wisdom and crafts. It is still standing today.

Parthenon

Assembly

City walls

MEDITERRANEAN SEA

CRETE

Crete was a base for pirates, who attacked and robbed merchant ships.

Pirate ship

The assembly was where Athenian citizens met to make big decisions about the city. People voted using clay discs.

19

Ancient China

Beginning in 475 BCE, China was divided into several kingdoms, which were always at war with each other. This era, called the Warring States period, ended in 221 BCE, when the king of Qin conquered all his rivals. He ruled as China's First Emperor. Qin, pronounced "Chin," gave its name to all of China.

Kingdoms at war

The many warring states each battled to become the most powerful. They were eventually united into the huge empire of China.

First Emperor of China

Ying Zheng, known as the First Emperor, ruled China harshly from 221–210 BCE. He forced everybody in the country to work for him. People had to build roads, canals, a great wall, and a huge tomb for him.

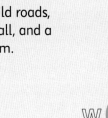

The First Emperor

The First Emperor built a road 500 miles (800 km) long, from Xianyang to Mongolia.

The Straight Road

Terra-cotta army

In 210 BCE, the First Emperor was buried beneath a human-made mountain. Nearby, an army of more than 7,000 life-size terra-cotta (clay) warriors was also buried.

Terra-cotta soldiers

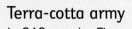

Xianyang

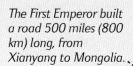

Epang palace

QIN

The capital of China was the city of Xianyang. The First Emperor built a palace here.

Chariot

Government officials traveled around in horse-drawn chariots.

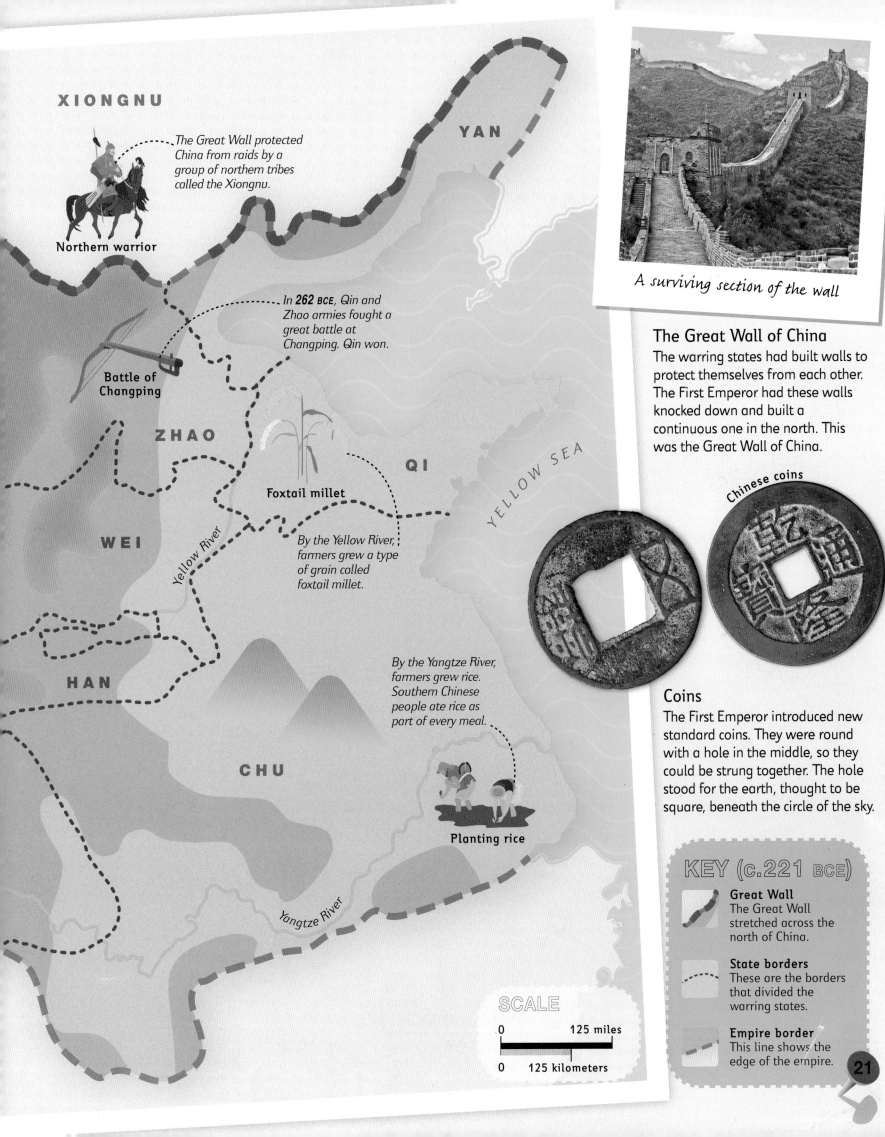

XIONGNU

The Great Wall protected China from raids by a group of northern tribes called the Xiongnu.

Northern warrior

YAN

A surviving section of the wall

In **262 BCE**, Qin and Zhao armies fought a great battle at Changping. Qin won.

Battle of Changping

ZHAO

QI

YELLOW SEA

Foxtail millet

By the Yellow River, farmers grew a type of grain called foxtail millet.

WEI

Yellow River

HAN

By the Yangtze River, farmers grew rice. Southern Chinese people ate rice as part of every meal.

CHU

Planting rice

Yangtze River

The Great Wall of China

The warring states had built walls to protect themselves from each other. The First Emperor had these walls knocked down and built a continuous one in the north. This was the Great Wall of China.

Chinese coins

Coins

The First Emperor introduced new standard coins. They were round with a hole in the middle, so they could be strung together. The hole stood for the earth, thought to be square, beneath the circle of the sky.

KEY (c.221 BCE)

Great Wall
The Great Wall stretched across the north of China.

State borders
These are the borders that divided the warring states.

Empire border
This line shows the edge of the empire.

SCALE

| 0 | 125 miles |

| 0 | 125 kilometers |

21

Ancient Rome

More than 2,000 years ago, ancient Rome was one of the most powerful nations in the world. At first, Rome was ruled by kings. It became a republic in 509 BCE, which meant that it was ruled by members of Roman society. In 27 BCE Rome became an empire, led by a ruler called an emperor. At its largest, in 117 CE, the Roman Empire was home to more than 65 million people.

Punic Wars

Between 264 and 146 BCE, Rome fought three wars against the city of Carthage, in modern-day Tunisia. Rome wanted control of the Mediterranean Sea. The wars, known as the Punic Wars, ended in total Roman victory.

General Hannibal from Carthage

KEY (c.117 CE)

 **Empire border**
The edge of the Roman Empire.

 Grain
Shipped to Rome from North Africa and Sicily.

Grapevines
Vines were planted across the empire to grow grapes to make into wine.

Timber
Forests were stripped of wood all over the empire.

Roman baths
Public bathing brought the Romans together.

Slaves
Many Romans owned slaves. Some slaves had to build Roman roads.

Amphitheaters
Open-air theaters entertained Romans across the empire.

Roman soldiers
The army kept the peace and defended the borders against enemy invasion.

Named after Emperor Hadrian, work on this wall began in 122 CE. It marked the northwest edge of the empire.

Hadrian's Wall

NORTH SEA

This leader of the Arverni tribe led an uprising against Roman power in 52 BCE.

The Romans built this lighthouse in what is now Spain.

Vercingetorix

This was the most important gold mine in the Roman Empire.

Tower of Hercules

Las Medulas

Pont du Gard

The Romans built aqueducts to transport water from one place to another.

ATLANTIC OCEAN

N
W   E
S

MEDITERRANEAN SEA

Carthaginians

The Carthaginians used war elephants to fight against the Roman Empire.

Julius Caesar

One of ancient Rome's most well-known leaders, Julius Caesar conquered large amounts of land for Rome. The empire began with his great-nephew, Augustus, who made himself the first emperor.

The Appian Way leading out of Rome

Roman roads

The Romans built many long, straight roads to link the towns and cities of the empire. These paved roads helped soldiers move quickly around the empire.

This famous amphitheater was built in *80 CE* to hold gladiator fights and other sports.

This impressive theater was used by the leaders of Rome, who made up the ruling Senate.

Theater of Pompey

Colosseum

Rome was said to have been founded by twins who were raised by a wolf.

Romulus and Remus

A massive wall was built around Rome in *271 CE*, called the Aurelian Wall.

This theater in Verona, Italy, is still in use today.

BLACK SEA

Emperor Constantine the Great ordered this column to be built in *330 CE*.

Verona Arena

Rome

Mount Vesuvius

Constantinople   **Column of Constantine**

The city of Pompeii was destroyed by the eruption of the volcano Mount Vesuvius in *79 CE*.

Theater at Djemila

The Romans built this amphitheater in what is now Tunisia.

Constantinople became the capital of the empire in *330 CE*. Walls were built around the city to help defend it against attacks.

These warships traveled all around the Mediterranean Sea.

Galley warship

Cleopatra ruled Egypt until *30 BCE*, when it was conquered by Rome.

An important city in Roman Libya.

Leptis Magna

Masada hill fort

In *74 CE*, a Jewish revolt against Roman rule ended when all the Jewish troops and civilians in the Masada fort killed themselves.

SCALE

0   200 miles

0   200 kilometers

Cleopatra

Judaism

The faith of the Jewish people, called Judaism, was the first religion that worshipped one God. Jews believe that God chose them as a special holy people and gave them a set of laws to follow.

Torah reading in a synagogue

Islam

Muslims worship a single God, called Allah. Every year, millions of Muslims travel to their holy city of Mecca in a special journey called the Hajj.

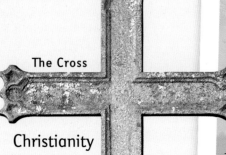

The Cross

Christianity

Christians believe in one God but also worship Jesus Christ as the Son of God. Jesus was a Jew who died 2,000 years ago, when he was nailed to a cross.

Christianity began in Jerusalem, where Jesus died.

Christianity

Jerusalem

Judaism

Judaism began in ancient Israel, the Jewish homeland.

Mecca

Islam

*Mecca, where the prophet Muhammad was born around **570 CE**, is the holiest city in Islam.*

Sikhism comes from northern India, where Guru Nanak was born.

Sikhism

Nankana Sahib

Lumbini

Hinduism

Buddhism

*Hinduism began in ancient India. Its sacred texts, the Vedas, were written down around **1200 BCE**.*

*Buddhism began in northeast India, where the Buddha was born in **563 BCE**.*

INDIAN OCEAN

African religious mask

World religions

A religion is a set of beliefs about how to live a good life and what happens after death. In the past, there were hundreds of different religions. Then, people began to follow larger, organized religions. Today, most people belong to only a few world religions.

Smaller religions

Alongside the major religions, there are still many smaller ones. In some parts of Africa, people believe in powerful spirits. They try to get the help of the spirits by dancing while wearing masks.

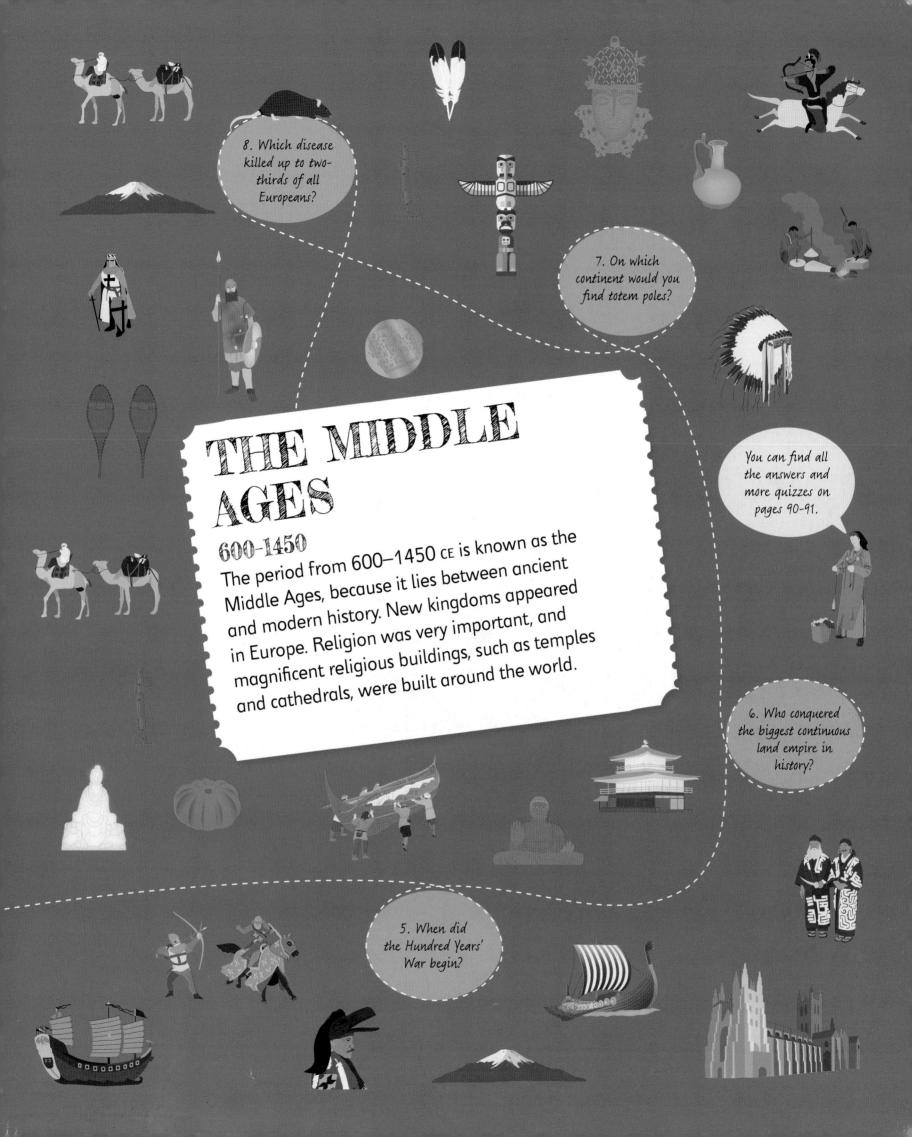

8. Which disease killed up to two-thirds of all Europeans?

7. On which continent would you find totem poles?

You can find all the answers and more quizzes on pages 90-91.

THE MIDDLE AGES

600-1450

The period from 600–1450 CE is known as the Middle Ages, because it lies between ancient and modern history. New kingdoms appeared in Europe. Religion was very important, and magnificent religious buildings, such as temples and cathedrals, were built around the world.

6. Who conquered the biggest continuous land empire in history?

5. When did the Hundred Years' War begin?

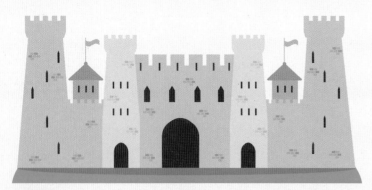

The Middle Ages

Many new kingdoms and empires arose during the Middle Ages. After the fall of the Roman Empire, several kingdoms appeared in Europe sharing a strong belief in Christianity. A new world religion also emerged during the Middle Ages: Islam.

250–950
Maya civilization
The Maya civilization, a collection of competing cities in Mesoamerica, is at its height.

Maya writing carved on bone

711–721
Muslim Spain
A North African Muslim army invades and conquers Spain. The Muslims then move into France but are defeated at the Battle of Poitiers in 732.

700
First American towns
The first towns are built in North America, in the eastern woodlands, by people known as the Mound Builders.

762
Baghdad
Caliph al-Mansur founds Baghdad as a new capital of the Islamic Empire, beginning the "Golden Age" of Islam.

1066
Norman Conquest
The Normans, under William the Conqueror, conquer England. To control their English subjects, they later build many castles.

William the Conqueror leading his men

1095–1099
First Crusade
The First Crusade is a holy war fought by European armies against the Muslims who rule the Holy Land. The crusaders capture Jerusalem, and start Christian kingdoms.

1200–1350
Mali Empire
Growth of the Mali Empire, which conquers Ghana. The capital, Timbuktu, is famed for its wealth and the learning of its Islamic scholars.

1206–1294
Mongol conquests
The Mongols of East Asia conquer an empire stretching from eastern Europe to the Pacific Ocean. It is the biggest continuous land empire in history.

1440–1473
Benin Empire founded
Reign of Oba (king) Ewuare the Great, founder of the Benin Empire of West Africa.

Queen Mother of Benin

1420–1446
Dome of Florence
The Italian architect Filippo Brunelleschi builds the dome of the cathedral in Florence.

Dome of Florence Cathedral

c.500–600
First West African State
Rise of the Kingdom of Ghana, the first known state in West Africa. Its wealth comes from gold, traded across the Sahara with North Africa.

622–632
Birth of Islam
In Arabia, Muhammad, the founder of Islam, unites the previously divided Arab tribes under his rule.

618–907
Tang dynasty
Under the Tang dynasty, the Chinese conquer a great empire, including much of Central Asia. Chang'an, the capital, is the world's biggest city.

Flag of Korea

668
Korea unified
King Munmu of Silla unites Korea, which was previously divided into separate kingdoms.

632–690
Arab conquests
The Arabs conquer the Persian Empire and North Africa.

Tang dynasty, model of a polo player

789
First Viking raid
The Vikings stage their first attack on Britain, beginning more than a century of raiding.

Viking axe and shield

800
Carolingian Empire
Pope Leo III crowns the Frankish (French) king, Charlemagne, as emperor. Charlemagne unites much of western Europe in his Carolingian Empire.

1050
Printing invented
Printing, with moveable clay type, is invented in China. Earlier Chinese books were printed using carved wooden blocks.

1000
Vikings reach America
Leif Erikson, a Viking explorer, sails to North America, which he calls Vinland.

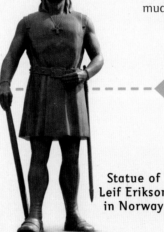

Statue of Leif Erikson in Norway

10th century
Arabic numerals
Arabic numerals (1,2,3, etc.) are first used in Europe. Invented in India, they are named after the Arabs who introduced them to Europe.

c.1270
First paper
People in Italy begin to make paper, at first from rags. Paper is much cheaper than parchment, which is made from animal skin.

Maori man from New Zealand

1280
Polynesians settle New Zealand
Polynesian sailors discover and settle New Zealand. After centuries of travel, it is the last place the Polynesians discover in the Pacific Ocean.

1289
First eyeglasses
Eyeglasses are invented in Italy and are used to help with reading.

1347–1352
Black Death
A terrible plague called the Black Death spreads from Asia across Europe. It kills between a third and two-thirds of the population.

Rat fleas spread the Black Death across Europe.

1337
Hundred Years' War begins
Beginning of the Hundred Years' War, a series of wars between England and France that went on for over a hundred years.

1315–1317
Great Famine
Cold, wet weather across northern Europe causes the Great Famine. Crops fail, and at least a tenth of the population starves to death.

The Vikings

From the 8th to the 11th centuries CE, the Vikings set off from Scandinavia to attack, trade, and settle in new lands. They sailed along the rivers of Russia to the Black Sea, and out into the North Sea and North Atlantic. They settled in the Faroe Islands, Iceland, and Greenland and became the first Europeans to reach America. In Britain, they conquered an area that the English called the Danelaw.

A rebuilt longhouse in Iceland

GREENLAND

ICELAND

KEY (890–1050)

Viking homelands
The areas in Scandinavia the Vikings came from.

Gains abroad
The areas that were taken by the Vikings.

 Viking voyages
The Vikings went on many voyages in their longships.

Battles and raids
The Vikings fought other people across Europe.

Settlements
Places where the Vikings settled down and had families.

Eric the Red

Eric the Red founded the first Viking settlement in Greenland in **985** CE.

Longhouse
A typical Viking home was a longhouse. It had one big shared room with a fire in the middle for warmth, cooking, and light. People slept on benches around the sides. Animals lived in a separate area at one end of the house.

N W E S

Leif Erikson sailed to North America around **1000** CE. He named the place he found Vinland.

Leif Erikson
VINLAND

ATLANTIC OCEAN

The Oseberg Ship

SCALE

0 — 500 miles

0 — 500 kilometers

Longships
Voyages were made in double-ended oak ships, with single square sails. Ships were so important to the Vikings that rulers were buried in them. This beautiful ship was found in a grave in Norway.

Across the sea
The Vikings sailed all around Europe and the Mediterranean, across Russia, the North Sea, and the North Atlantic.

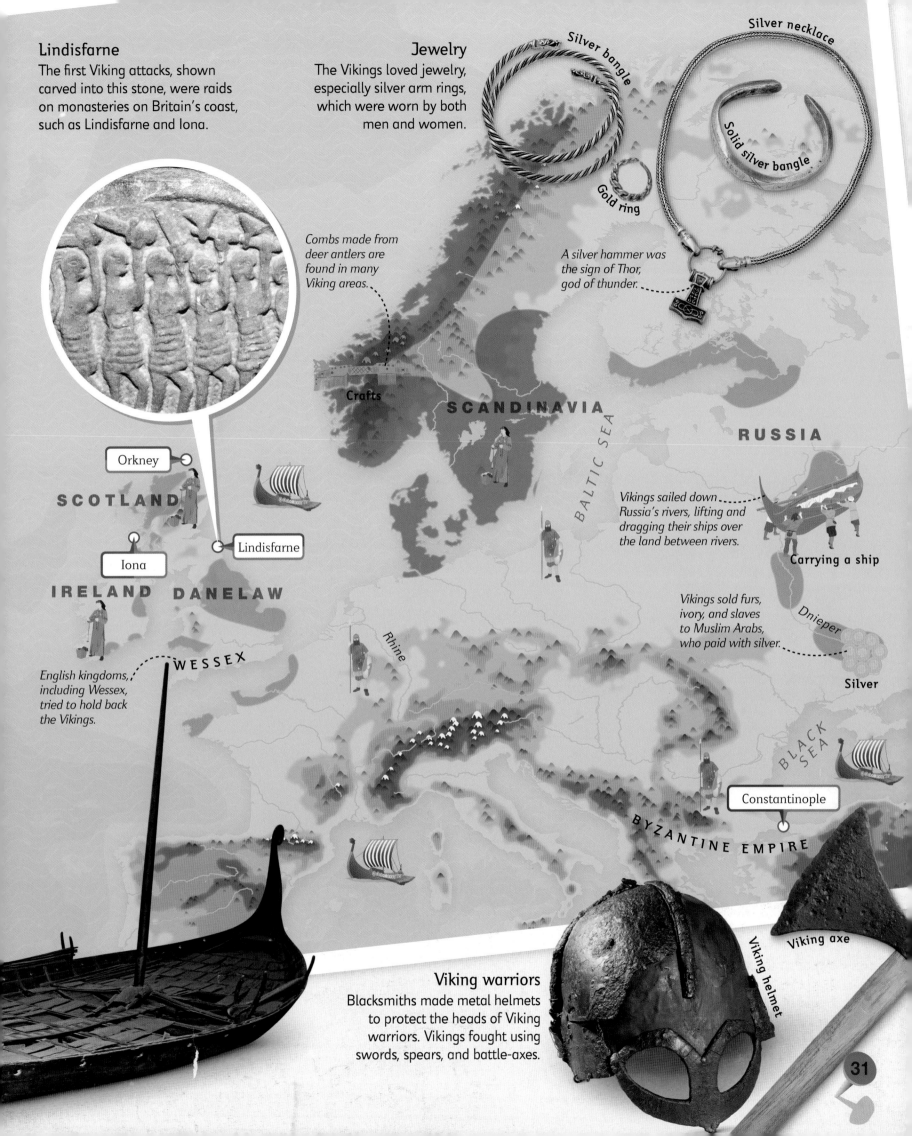

Lindisfarne
The first Viking attacks, shown carved into this stone, were raids on monasteries on Britain's coast, such as Lindisfarne and Iona.

Jewelry
The Vikings loved jewelry, especially silver arm rings, which were worn by both men and women.

Silver bangle

Silver necklace

Solid silver bangle

Gold ring

Combs made from deer antlers are found in many Viking areas.

A silver hammer was the sign of Thor, god of thunder.

Crafts

SCANDINAVIA

BALTIC SEA

RUSSIA

Orkney

SCOTLAND

Lindisfarne

Iona

IRELAND   DANELAW

Vikings sailed down Russia's rivers, lifting and dragging their ships over the land between rivers.

Carrying a ship

Vikings sold furs, ivory, and slaves to Muslim Arabs, who paid with silver.

Dnieper

Silver

English kingdoms, including Wessex, tried to hold back the Vikings.

WESSEX

Rhine

BLACK SEA

Constantinople

BYZANTINE EMPIRE

Viking helmet

Viking axe

Viking warriors
Blacksmiths made metal helmets to protect the heads of Viking warriors. Vikings fought using swords, spears, and battle-axes.

31

Bulguksa Temple

Bulguksa Temple
The kingdom of Silla started following the Buddhist religion in 527 CE. The Bulguksa Temple was built in Gyeongju, the royal capital, in 751–774 CE. Bulguksa means "temple of the land of Buddha."

Coastal kingdoms
Korea is an area of land that sticks out from Asia into the Pacific Ocean. It traded a lot with nearby China.

Silla crown
In the Silla capital, Gyeongju, kings were buried in tombs covered with mounds of rocks. The tombs contained rich treasures, such as gold crowns decorated with antler or tree shapes.

KEY (500 CE)

Goods leaving the empire

Goguryeo
The kingdom that Korea is named after.

Baekje
Known for its statues and jewelry.

Gaya
A small group of independent cities.

Silla
The most powerful Korean kingdom.

Goguryeo sold luxuries such as fur, gold, and silver to China.

Furs

Gold

Silver

N W S E

Goguryeo men hunted deer on horseback using bows.

Pyongyang

Hunter on horseback

YELLOW SEA

SEA OF JAPAN

Baekje sculptors made smiling statues of the Buddha.

Buddha statues

Tomb of King Suro

Gyeongju

Kings of Gaya were buried beneath big mounds of earth.

Gwangju

Ancient Korea

By the first century BCE, there were three competing kingdoms in Korea. Goguryeo was a large kingdom in the north; Baekje was in the southwest; and Silla was in the southeast. There was also a group of independent cities in the south called Gaya. Silla conquered the other kingdoms in 668 CE, but modern Korea took its name from the kingdom of Goguryeo.

SCALE
0   100 miles

0   100 kilometers

Ancient Japan

Between the fourth and sixth centuries CE, Japan's many small territories were united into one country under an emperor. Japan's emperors said they were descended from the goddess of the sun. Japan used Chinese writing and began to follow Buddhism, which mixed with the local religion of Shinto.

Emperor Kanmu (ruled 781–806 CE)

God-like emperor
Japan has the world's oldest royal family. It has reigned for at least 1,500 years and continues up to the present day. The emperors were thought to be like gods, so only they could rule the country.

Island state
Japan lies off the east coast of Asia. It is made up of four main islands: Honshu, Hokkaido, Shikoku, and Kyushu.

SCALE

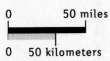

0   50 miles

0   50 kilometers

The native people of Hokkaido are called the Ainu.

Ainu people

Hokkaido

PACIFIC OCEAN

Samurai warriors wore elaborate suits of armor.

Samurai armor

SEA OF JAPAN

The Todai-ji Temple in Nara has a 49 ft (15 m) tall statue of the Buddha.

Shinto shrine

The Japanese traditional religion, Shinto, is based on the worship of spirits called kami.

Honshu

Edo

Mount Fuji

Mount Fuji is a holy mountain, worshipped as a Shinto spirit.

Kinkaku-ji is a famous Buddhist temple built in 1397.

Kyoto

Todai-ji buddha

Nara

Kinkaku-ji

Himeji

Shikoku

Kyushu

Himeji castle
Wealthy Japanese noblemen lived in castles, where they had their own followings of warriors called samurai. This castle in Himeji was originally built in the 1330s.

Inuit hunter carrying a kayak

Inuit

The Inuit, the people of the icy Arctic, lived by catching fish and hunting seals, whales, and walruses. The Inuit chased these animals in light sealskin boats called kayaks.

Homes

People in different areas had different kinds of homes. This photograph, taken in 1876, shows a Paiute village in the Great Basin area. These huts, made from sticks, are called wickiups.

Indigenous people of North America

Before Europeans settled in North America, it was home to hundreds of groups of indigenous (native) people. North America can be divided into ten different regions, called cultural areas. In each area, people shared similar ways of life. In some places, they farmed, while in others they lived by hunting.

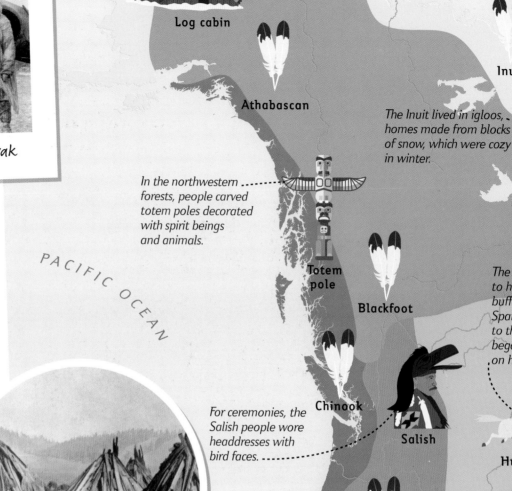

The Athabascan people of the subarctic lived in big log cabins.

Log cabin

Athabascan

BEAUFORT SEA

Inuit

The Inuit lived in igloos, homes made from blocks of snow, which were cozy in winter.

Igloo

In the northwestern forests, people carved totem poles decorated with spirit beings and animals.

Totem pole

Chipewyan

Blackfoot

The plains were home to huge herds of buffalo. When the Spanish brought horses to the Americas, people began to hunt buffalo on horseback.

Chinook

For ceremonies, the Salish people wore headdresses with bird faces.

Salish

Hunting buffalo

Paiute

Crow

Shoshone

Cheyenne

Wickiup shelter

Wickiups were made from sticks. They were easy to build quickly.

Apache

Comanche

PACIFIC OCEAN

N W E S

Varied landscape

North America has many different habitats, with snow in the north and grasslands in the center. Native peoples lived in all these areas.

SCALE

0   500 miles

0   500 kilometers

KEY (1500)

Indigenous peoples
Some of the groups who lived across North America.

Arctic
This is the coldest region, where no trees grow.

Subarctic
Trees grew in the subarctic, but it was still cold and snowy.

Plains
This region was home to flat, treeless grasslands.

Eastern woodlands
These areas had thick forests.

Southwest
The hottest, driest region.

Southeast
A hot, wet region with forests and swamps.

Great Basin
The Great Basin had mountains, river valleys, and open plains.

Northwest coast
A forested region with mild, wet weather.

Plateau
An area surrounded by high mountain ranges.

California
Home to grasslands, wooded hills, and river valleys.

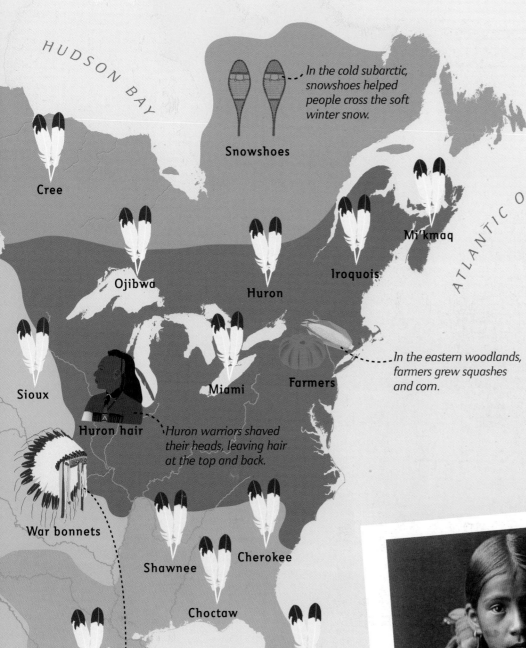

BAFFIN BAY

HUDSON BAY

ATLANTIC OCEAN

In the cold subarctic, snowshoes helped people cross the soft winter snow.

Snowshoes

Cree

Ojibwa

Huron

Mi'kmaq

Iroquois

Sioux

Miami

Farmers

In the eastern woodlands, farmers grew squashes and corn.

Huron hair

Huron warriors shaved their heads, leaving hair at the top and back.

War bonnets

Shawnee

Cherokee

Choctaw

Natchez

Seminole

On the plains, warriors wore war bonnets made from eagle feathers.

Apache women

The Apache lived in the hot, dry Southwest. An Apache woman or girl would spend her time gathering wild plants for food, including prickly pears, roots, and seeds. This Apache girl was photographed in 1905.

Apache girl

35

African empires

Since around 100 CE, powerful kingdoms have risen and fallen in the land south of the huge Sahara Desert in Africa. These kingdoms struggled to gain land and control of trade routes. Trading made rulers rich, especially through selling gold, ivory, and slaves. In addition to rich monarchs, there were many ordinary farmers in the forests and grasslands below the Sahara.

Islam

North African traders crossed the Sahara Desert on camels to trade with Mali. They brought their religion, Islam, with them. In the ninth century, the people of Mali became Muslims. The Great Mosque of Djenné is the largest mud-brick building in the world.

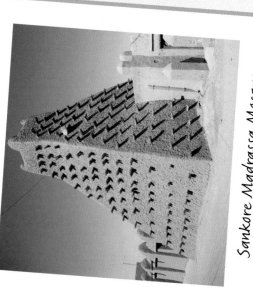

Timbuktu

The city of Timbuktu in West Africa was famous for being rich. Gold was mined from local goldfields and traded for other goods. Timbuktu was also a center of learning. There were three mosques where people could study. Sankore Madrassa Mosque was built in the 14th century.

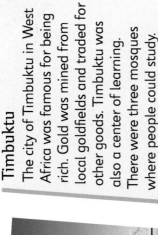

Sankore Madrassa Mosque

African powers

The great African empires and kingdoms were to the south of the Sahara Desert, which stretches across North Africa.

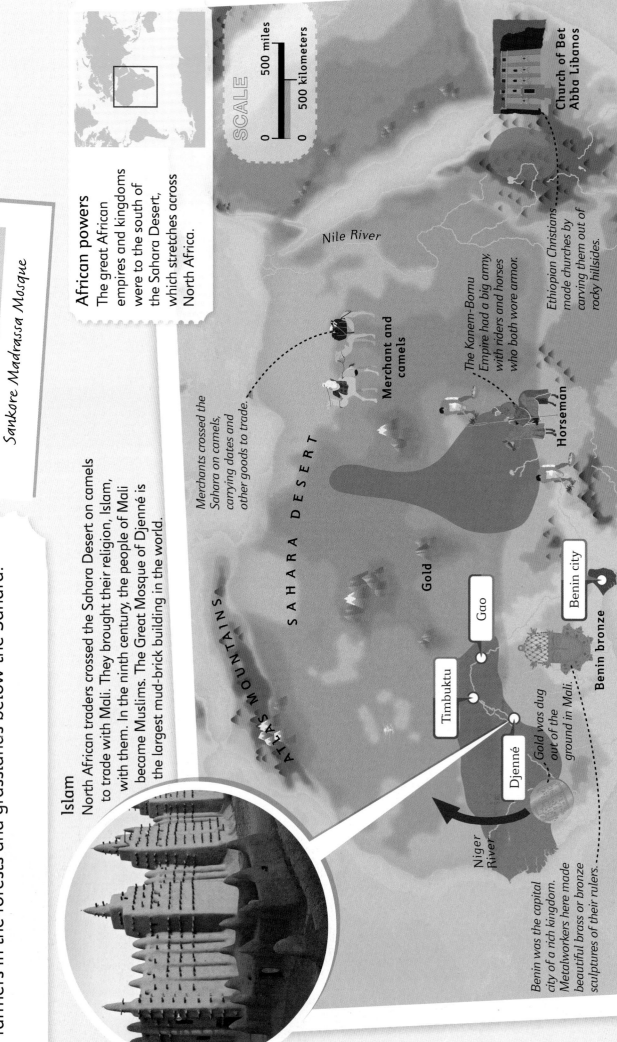

Nile River

SCALE

0 ___ 500 miles

0 ___ 500 kilometers

Church of Bet Abba Libanos

Merchants crossed the Sahara on camels, carrying dates and other goods to trade.

Merchant and camels

The Kanem-Bornu Empire had a big army, with riders and horses who both wore armor.

Horseman

Ethiopian Christians made churches by carving them out of rocky hillsides.

S A H A R A   D E S E R T

A T L A S   M O U N T A I N S

Gold

Gao

Timbuktu

Djenné

Gold was dug out of the ground in Mali.

Benin city

Benin bronze

Benin was the capital city of a rich kingdom. Metalworkers here made beautiful brass or bronze sculptures of their rulers.

Niger River

King Ezana's Stela

CONGO BASIN

African craft workers were skilled at making iron tools to trade.

Crafts

INDIAN OCEAN

DRAKENSBERG

ATLANTIC OCEAN

N
W E
S

Great Zimbabwe

These mysterious stone ruins are part of Great Zimbabwe. This city is said to have been home to 18,000 people in the 11th to 15th centuries. Great Zimbabwe grew rich from trading in iron, copper, salt, gold, and ivory (elephant tusk).

KEY (c. 1400)

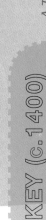

Trade routes

Mali Empire
This empire lasted from 1230 to 1670.

Kingdom of Zimbabwe
This kingdom lasted from 1220 to 1450.

Kingdom of Benin
This kingdom lasted from 1180 to 1897.

Bunyoro–Kitara Empire
This empire lasted from the 1500s to 1894.

Ethiopian Empire
This empire lasted from 1137 to 1974.

Kingdom of Kongo
This kingdom lasted from 1390 to 1974.

Kanem–Bornu Empire
This empire lasted from the 800s to 1900.

Farming
Farmers grew vegetables, such as yams, or grains, such as millet.

Aksum

The earliest African kingdom was Aksum in Ethiopia, which lasted from around 100 CE to 940 CE. Aksum's riches came from trading goods by sea with Egypt and Arabia. Early kings of Aksum built tall stone grave markers, called stelae. King Ezana had this one put up in the fourth century.

King Alvaro of Kongo in 1642

King of Kongo

In the 1480s, West African kings began trading with Europeans, such as the Portuguese. The kings of Kongo became Christians and even took Portuguese names. This picture shows King Alvaro meeting Dutch visitors.

The Silk Road

The trade route that allowed merchants to travel from east to west from Asia to Europe was known as the Silk Road. This road was first set up around 200 BCE and lasted until sea routes across the Indian Ocean replaced it in the 1500s CE. In addition to goods for trading, new ideas, religions, and inventions traveled along the Silk Road.

East to west

The Silk Road began in China. It stretched through the mountains and deserts of central Asia to the eastern Mediterranean Sea.

Marco Polo

In 1271 the young Italian Marco Polo traveled along the Silk Road to China with his father and uncle, who were both merchants. He wrote a best-selling account of his travels when he returned home 24 years later.

Marco Polo

Caravanserais

Merchants traveling along the Silk Road stopped off in caravanserais, or inns. Here they could eat and sleep and let their animals rest.

A historic caravanserai in Lebanon

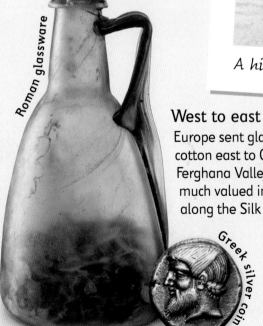

Roman glassware

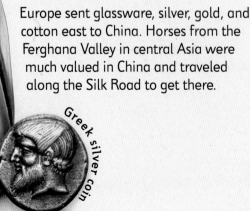

Greek silver coin

West to east

Europe sent glassware, silver, gold, and cotton east to China. Horses from the Ferghana Valley in central Asia were much valued in China and traveled along the Silk Road to get there.

Horses were used to pull carts where the roads were good enough.

Horses and carts

BLACK SEA

Roman merchant ship

MEDITERRANEAN SEA

Transporting goods by sea was quicker and cheaper, but also more dangerous.

RED SEA

KEY (220 CE)

Main trade route
This was the path that most travelers and merchants followed on their journeys between east and west.

- Gold
- Silver
- Glassware
- Cotton
- Grapes
- Figs
- Walnuts
- Ferghana horses

- Jade
- Porcelain
- Paper
- Gunpowder
- Tea
- Sugar
- Spices
- Silk
- Salt

East to west

China sent silk, porcelain, jade, tea, and spices west along the Silk Road toward Europe. Among the many inventions that traveled west were paper and gunpowder.

Chinese porcelain

Chinese tea leaves

Chinese silk clothing

SCALE

0   500 miles

0   500 kilometers

CASPIAN SEA

Missionaries traveled to Asia in **781 CE** to spread the Christian religion.

Christian missionaries

Buddhist monks spread their religion from India to China in the **first century** CE.

Camel trains

Buddhist monks

Trains (groups) of two-humped camels transported travelers and goods along the Silk Road.

ARABIAN SEA

N W E S

Arab dhow

These traditional Arab sailing ships carried goods across the Indian Ocean and into the Persian Gulf.

Huge fleets of ships called junks sailed across the Indian Ocean.

Chinese junk

INDIAN OCEAN

The Middle Ages

During the Middle Ages, Europe was made up of many kingdoms. This was a period when noblemen lived in castles and fought in wars, riding into battle as knights on horseback. The Christian Church was rich and powerful, building great cathedrals across Europe.

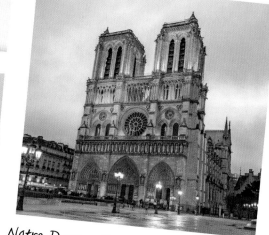

Notre Dame, France, founded in 1163

Stained glass image of Joan of Arc

Cathedrals around Europe

The biggest buildings in medieval Europe were cathedrals. These were big churches where archbishops based their power. Some cathedrals held the body parts of saints, called relics. People traveled on long journeys, called pilgrimages, to visit these relics.

Joan of Arc

From 1337 to 1453, England and France fought a war, later called the Hundred Years' War. Joan of Arc, a peasant girl, helped lead the French to victory.

Canterbury Cathedral contained the bones of the saint Thomas Becket.

SCOTLAND

IRELAND

ENGLAND

Canterbury Cathedral

*France and England fought for over 100 years in this war, from **1337–1453**.*

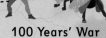

100 Years' War

European castles

Kings and nobles built hundreds of castles across Europe. They used them as bases to fight wars against each other and to rule over the local people.

ATLANTIC OCEAN

Avignon

FRANCE

PORTUGAL

ARAGON

CASTILE

EMIRATE OF GRANADA

Castle Hohenzollern in Germany

0 — 200 miles

0 — 200 kilometers

Power struggles
The countries of medieval Europe fought over land but shared a strong belief in the Christian religion.

Peasants farming, late 15th century

The Teutonic Knights were a brotherhood of Christian warriors.

NORWAY

Bergen

SWEDEN

Teutonic Knight

Hanseatic ship

The Hanseatic League was a group of trading towns in Germany, Poland, and Scandinavia that controlled sea trade.

In the 13th century, the Mongols from Asia conquered a huge empire.

Bremen

Charles IV was the head of the Holy Roman Empire from 1346–1378.

Emperor Charles IV

HOLY ROMAN EMPIRE

POLAND

KHANATE OF THE GOLDEN HORDE

Mongol warrior

HUNGARY

VENICE

GENOA

FLORENCE

Rome

BLACK SEA

BYZANTINE EMPIRE

SERBIA

OTTOMAN EMPIRE

SICILY

MEDITERRANEAN SEA

Peasants in the Middle Ages
Most people lived as poor peasants, farming the land for the rich. Many were serfs, who were not free. They worked for a lord in exchange for land to grow their own food on.

KEY (c.1400)

VENICE — **City-states**
Some powerful cities became tiny countries in their own right.

Borders
These lines show the borders between countries.

Cogs
Merchant ships called cogs carried the Black Death to Europe's ports

Black Death
The plague spread in these regions, carried by rat fleas.

Black Death
In the 1340s, the Black Death, a deadly disease carried by rat fleas, arrived in Europe. It spread quickly across the whole continent and killed between a third and two-thirds of Europe's population.

Black Death burial scene, 1349

41

1. Which South American empire made its leaders into mummies?

2. Who built India's Jama Masjid?

3. What was Istanbul called before the Ottomans renamed it?

4. What was the name of Vasco da Gama's ship?

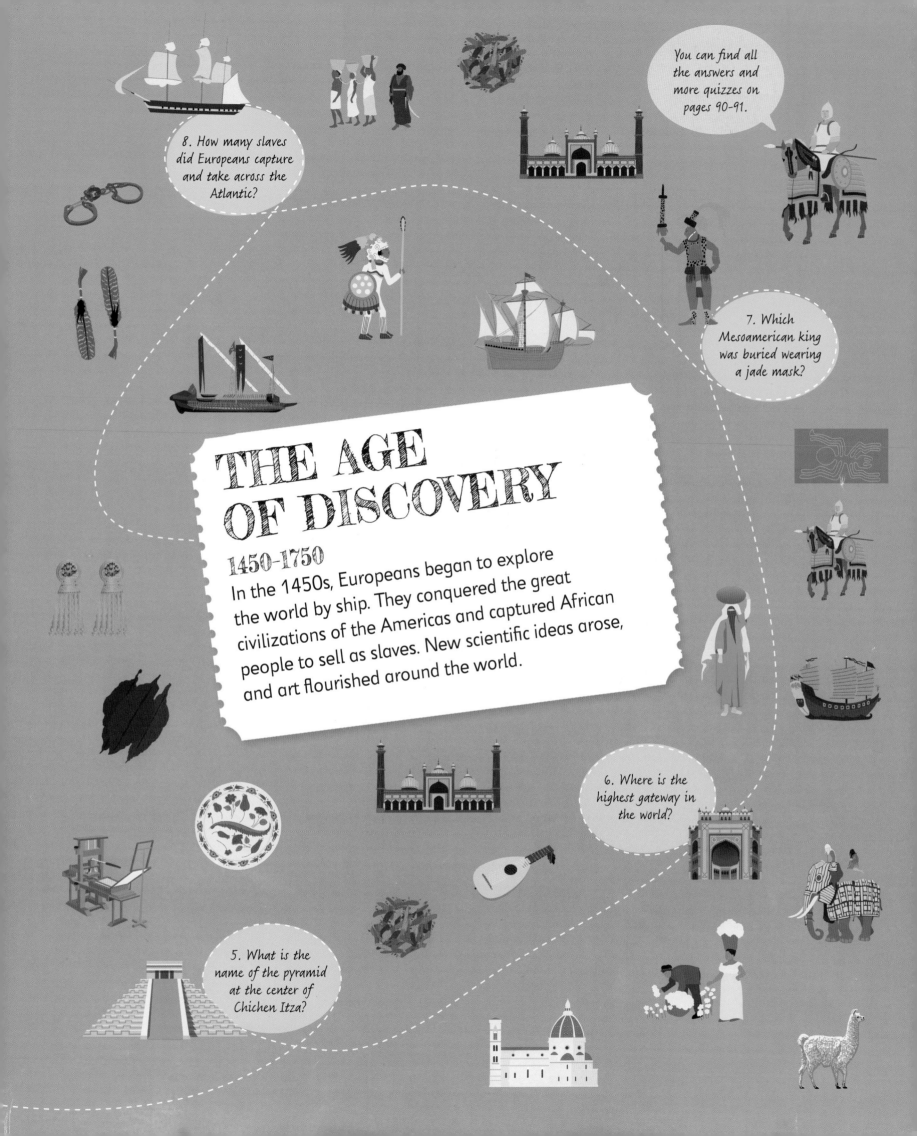

The age of discovery

In the 1450s, big changes began that would bring the Middle Ages to an end. European ships set off on voyages of exploration around the world. There were scientific discoveries and new ideas, which were shared across the continent in printed books. Europeans became the most powerful people in the world, yet they were divided because of religious differences.

1452
Portuguese enslave Africans
The Portuguese begin to use African slave labor in their sugar plantations in Madeira.

1497–1498
Portuguese reach India
The Portuguese explorer Vasco da Gama sails to India and back.

Vasco da Gama's ship

1525
Inca Empire
The Inca Empire of Peru is at its height.

The Incas used llamas to carry things for them...

1520–1566
Suleiman the Magnificent
Reign of Suleiman the Magnificent, the most famous Ottoman sultan.

1519–1522
World voyage
Ferdinand Magellan leads a Spanish expedition in the first crossing of the Pacific. One of his ships sails on to make the first voyage around the world.

1529
Siege of Vienna
Suleiman the Magnificent lays siege to Vienna, capital of Austria, but is not able to capture the city. The Ottoman advance into Europe is stopped.

1532
Conquest of the Incas
Spaniards, led by Francisco Pizarro, conquer the South American Inca Empire.

1534
Church of England founded
In England King Henry VIII argues with the Pope and declares himself head of the new Church of England.

King Henry VIII

1631–1648
Taj Mahal
The Mughal emperor Shah Jahan builds the Taj Mahal, in memory of his favorite wife, Mumtaz Mahal.

Taj Mahal

1619
African slaves in North America
The first African slaves are brought to North America by the English.

1453
Ottomans capture Constantinople
Ottoman Turks capture Constantinople, rename it Istanbul, and make it their capital.

A book printed by Gutenberg

1455
First European printed book
Johannes Gutenberg, inventor of the printing press, creates the first printed book in Europe. The invention spreads, and by 1500, 20 million books have been printed.

1488
Portuguese sail around Africa
The Portuguese explorer Bartolomeu Dias sails around the southern tip of Africa, which he names the "Cape of Good Hope." Europeans can now sail to India.

1497
English reach Newfoundland
John Cabot, an Italian, leads an English voyage to Newfoundland in North America.

1493
Spanish found Hispaniola
Columbus founds the first European settlement in the Americas, La Isabela on Hispaniola in the Caribbean.

Christopher Columbus

1492
Columbus reaches the Americas
The Italian Christopher Columbus sails from Spain across the Atlantic and reaches the Americas, which Europeans did not know about before.

1500
Portuguese reach Brazil
Pedro Cabral leads a fleet from Portugal to India, reaching Brazil on the way, which he claims for Portugal.

1501–1504
Michelangelo's _David_
In Florence, the Italian artist Michelangelo carves his famous sculpture of David.

1510
Transatlantic slave trade
The Spanish take 50 African slaves to Hispaniola, beginning the transatlantic slave trade.

1519–1521
Spaniards conquer the Aztecs
A group of Spaniards led by Hernan Cortes conquers the Aztec Empire of Mexico.

1517
The church divides
In Germany, Martin Luther challenges the teachings of the church, leading to a later split between Protestants and Catholics.

1516–1517
Rise of the Ottoman Empire
Ottoman Turks conquer Arabia, Syria, and Egypt.

1534–1542
French reach Canada
The French explorer Jacques Cartier makes three voyages to Canada, which he claims for France.

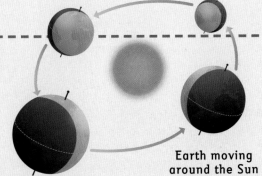

Earth moving around the Sun

1543
Copernicus says the earth moves around the sun
Polish astronomer Nicolas Copernicus argues that the earth goes around the sun rather than the other way around.

1609–1616
Blue Mosque
The Ottoman sultan, Ahmed I, builds the Blue Mosque in Istanbul.

1607
English settle in North America
The English found Jamestown in Virginia, beginning their settlement of North America.

1588
Spanish Armada defeated
During a war with Protestant England, Catholic Spain sends an armada (fleet of ships) to invade England, but it is defeated.

Queen Elizabeth 1 of England

Aztec and Maya civilizations

Mesoamerica (meaning "middle America") was home to the Maya. They lived in many cities ruled by kings who fought each other. Their civilization was at its height between 300 and 900 CE. Later, in the 16th century, the Aztecs of Mexico conquered a great empire. Both peoples built cities with tall, pyramid-shaped temples.

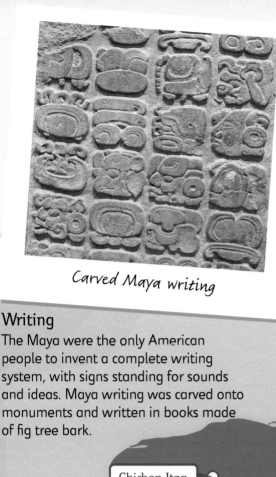

Carved Maya writing

Writing
The Maya were the only American people to invent a complete writing system, with signs standing for sounds and ideas. Maya writing was carved onto monuments and written in books made of fig tree bark.

GULF OF MEXICO

Tlacopan

Tenochtitlan

Tetzcoco

Cholula

Aztec warriors wore colorful costumes, dressing as eagles and jaguars.

The Olmecs, an earlier civilization, carved huge stone heads starting around **900 BCE**.

Chichen Itza

El Castillo

A stepped pyramid, El Castillo, is at the center of the Maya city of Chichen Itza, built around **600 CE**.

At their Great Temple in Tenochtitlan, the Aztecs killed prisoners as sacrifices (offerings) to the gods.

Great Temple at Tenochtitlan

Aztec warrior

Olmec heads

Palenque

Bonompak

Yaxchilan

Tikal

Copan

Tehuantepec

Maya kings were seen as living gods. King Pacal of Palenque was buried beneath a pyramid-shaped temple, wearing a jade mask.

Maya king

KEY

Aztec Empire
The greatest extent of the Aztec Empire.

Maya region
The area under the influence of Maya cities.

Goods coming in
Conquered people had to send gifts to their Aztec rulers.

Cocoa
Cocoa beans were used to make a hot chocolate drink.

Feathers
Colorful feathers were of great value.

Between continents
The Aztecs and Maya lived in Mesoamerica, which lies between North and South America. "Meso" means "middle."

PACIFIC OCEAN

SCALE

0   100 miles

0   100 kilometers

Emperor Atahualpa

Inca emperor

Emperors, called Sapa Incas, were said to be descended from the sun god. They were seen as living gods. When Inca emperors died, their bodies were preserved as mummies.

Inca terraces

Terraces

The Incas solved the problem of growing food on steep mountainsides by building flat, raised strips of earth called terraces. They grew potatoes, quinoa, and other crops.

Inca Empire

The 16th-century Inca Empire, in the high Andes Mountains of Peru, was the biggest and best organized empire in America. The emperor was at the top of Inca society. Under him were thousands of officials, then millions of ordinary people who worked as farmers, soldiers, and builders.

Ruins of Machu Picchu

The town of Machu Picchu was built 1.6 miles (2.7 km) above sea level, high in the Andes Mountains.

The Incas conquered the Chimu people in the 1470s. The Chimu were skilled at working in gold.

Chimu gold

Chan Chan

Nazca people made huge drawings in the desert.

Machu Picchu

Nazca carvings

Cuzco

Inca walls used huge blocks carved into different shapes, which fit tightly together.

Nazca

Cuzco walls

Lake Titicaca

PACIFIC OCEAN

Llamas were kept for wool, meat, dung (which was burned as fuel), and to carry loads.

Llamas

The Inca improved old roads and built new ones to make a network 24,800 miles (39,900 km) long.

N W E S

SCALE

0 — 250 miles

0 — 250 kilometers

High empire

The Inca Empire ran for 2,500 miles (4,000 km) down the west coast of South America. Much of it was high up in the Andes mountain range.

Voyages of discovery

In the 15th century, an age of discovery began, with explorers setting off on long sea journeys. The earliest voyages were made by the Chinese in the early 1400s. Later, European explorers searching for a new sea route to Asia found America instead.

KEY

Zheng He's seven voyages, 1405–1433.

Christopher Columbus's voyage, 1492.

Vasco da Gama's voyage, 1497–1498.

John Cabot's voyage, 1497.

Ferdinand Magellan's voyage, 1519–1521.

John Cabot sailed the Matthew to North America.

John Cabot, like Columbus, hoped to get to Asia by sailing west in 1497.

ENGLAND

The *Matthew*

John Cabot

SPAIN

PORTUGAL

Hoping to reach Asia, Columbus sailed the Santa Maria to the Caribbean.

The *Santa Maria*

NORTH AMERICA

ATLANTIC OCEAN

Mapping the world

This map shows what Europeans thought the world looked like in 1491. Europe is on the left and Asia is on the right. There is no America because Europeans had not discovered it yet.

15th-century map

SOUTH AMERICA

São Gabriel

Vasco da Gama sailed to India and back in the São Gabriel.

PACIFIC OCEAN

SOUTHERN OCEAN

ARCTIC OCEAN

In **1497**, Vasco da Gama sailed from Portugal to India.

Christopher Columbus sailed from Spain to the Caribbean in **1492**.

In **1519**, Ferdinand Magellan sailed from Spain to the Pacific.

Vasco da Gama

Christopher Columbus

Ferdinand Magellan

Death of Magellan

Ferdinand Magellan led the first ever crossing of the Pacific Ocean. When he reached Mactan Island in April 1521, he was killed in a battle with local people.

Magellan being attacked

OTTOMAN EMPIRE

PERSIAN EMPIRE

MUGHAL EMPIRE

ARABIA

AFRICA

Zheng He was a Chinese admiral who led seven voyages to explore south Asia and east Africa.

Zheng He

MING EMPIRE

PACIFIC OCEAN

THE PHILIPPINES

Magellan's death in the Philippines didn't stop his crew from continuing their voyage of discovery.

THE SPICE ISLANDS

Zheng He sailed with fleets of huge ships called junks.

Chinese junk ship

INDIAN OCEAN

The *Victoria*

The Victoria was the only one of Magellan's five ships to complete the voyage.

The spice routes

One of the main aims of European explorers was to find new spices. These included pepper from India and nutmeg and cloves from the Spice Islands. They could be sold for great sums of money back in Europe.

Nutmeg

Cloves

Black pepper

The Mughal Empire

In the 1520s, a ruler from central Asia called Babur invaded India. His empire made scientific breakthroughs, including new stargazing technology. The Mughals ruled most of India before it was taken over by Britain in 1857.

Mughal founder

Babur had conquered and lost lands in central Asia before he successfully founded the Mughal Empire. He wrote a book about his life called the *Baburnama*, which described his military conquests.

Babur in a scene from the Baburnama

Mountain to ocean

Over the centuries, the Mughal Empire grew from a small kingdom to an empire reaching all the way from the Himalayas to the Indian Ocean.

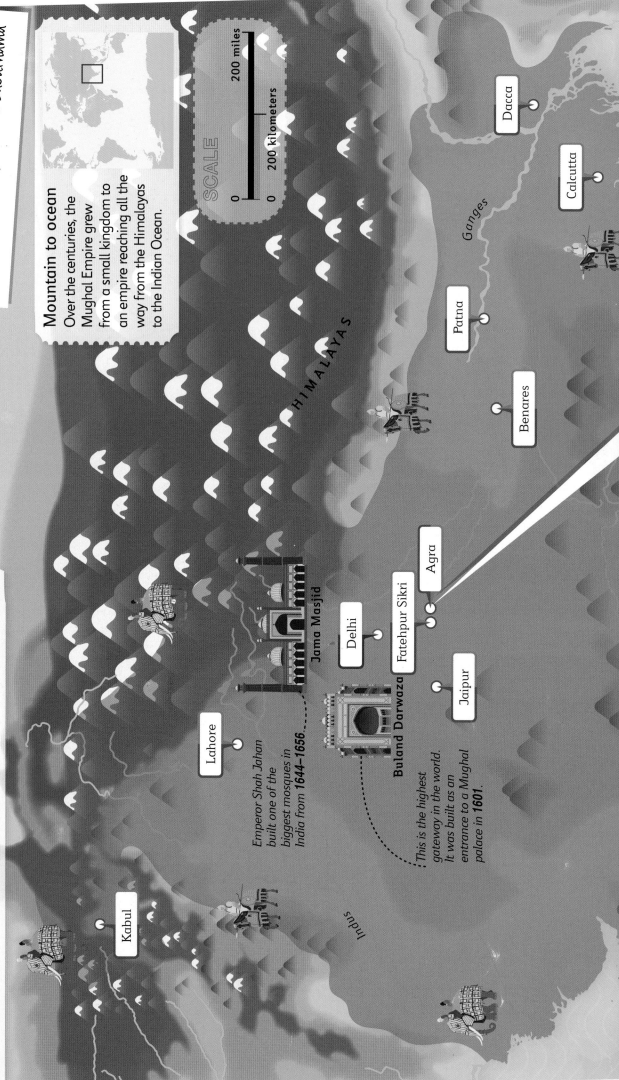

SCALE

0   200 miles

0   200 kilometers

Dacca

Calcutta

Ganges

Patna

Benares

HIMALAYAS

Jama Masjid

Delhi

Agra

Fatehpur Sikri

Buland Darwaza

Jaipur

Lahore

Emperor Shah Jahan built one of the biggest mosques in India from 1644–1656.

This is the highest gateway in the world. It was built as an entrance to a Mughal palace in 1601.

Kabul

Indus

Taj Mahal

The Taj Mahal—which means "crown of the palace"—was built by Mughal emperor Shah Jahan (1628–1658) to hold the tomb of his favorite wife, Mumtaz Mahal. Mughal buildings often had onion-shaped domes.

Cinnamon

Ginger

Turmeric

Cardamom

BAY OF BENGAL

Europeans in India

In 1498, Portuguese explorer Vasco da Gama sailed to India, which was little known in Europe. The spices he brought back encouraged many more Europeans to travel to India.

INDIA

Surat

Bombay

Goa

Madras

Pondicherry

Calicut

Cochin

CEYLON

ARABIAN SEA

The Portuguese were the first Europeans to sail to India. Other Europeans followed.

Portuguese ship

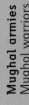

Rise and fall

The empire reached its largest size under the sixth Mughal emperor, Aurangzeb (1658–1707). He took over many lands and ruled over 160 million people. These lands were lost after his death.

Aurangzeb as a young man

Dhow

Arab and Indian traders crossed the seas in ships called dhows, which had large triangular sails.

KEY (c. 1700)

Akbar's empire
Akbar (1556–1605) made Babur's empire bigger by conquering many lands.

Southern conquests
Southern India was conquered by Emperor Aurangzeb between the 1650s and 1680s.

Mughal armies
Mughal warriors fought battles to gain land or defend the empire.

Mughal war elephant
Elephants were used in Mughal battles.

N E W S

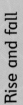

The Ottoman Empire

Between 1300 and 1699, the Ottoman Turks conquered a vast empire, which stretched from North Africa to the Indian Ocean. At the empire's height, more than 35 million people lived under Ottoman rulers, called sultans.

KEY (c.1566)

Goods coming into the empire

Furs
Luxurious furs were bought from icy Russia.

Slaves
Slaves did many jobs, from paperwork to guarding the sultan.

Spices
Used to flavor food.

Incense
Burning incense released perfume.

Silk
Raw silk was made into fine cloth.

Belgrade

TYRRHENIAN SEA

Tunis

Algiers

TUNISIA

ALGERIA

Ottoman galley

Ottoman warships, called galleys, were rowed by prisoners, who were chained to benches.

Tripoli

TRIPOLI

Istanbul
In 1453, the Ottomans conquered Constantinople. It was renamed Istanbul, which means "in the city." Istanbul's Blue Mosque was built by Sultan Ahmed between 1609 and 1616.

Empire founder
The word "Ottoman" comes from the name of the first ruler, Osman I. He founded a small state in northern Anatolia in the early 1300s.

The Blue Mosque

Osman I, ruled 1299–1324

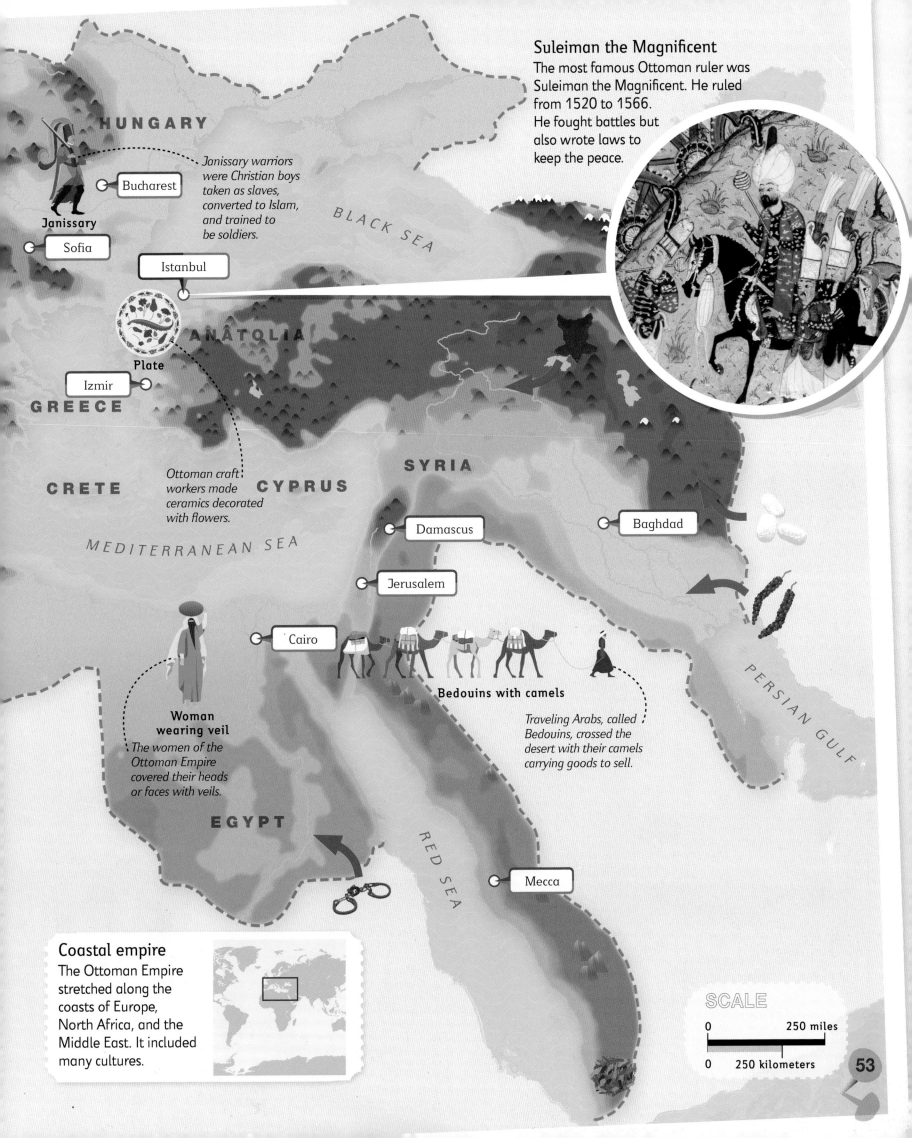

HUNGARY

Janissary

Janissary warriors were Christian boys taken as slaves, converted to Islam, and trained to be soldiers.

Bucharest

Sofia

BLACK SEA

Suleiman the Magnificent
The most famous Ottoman ruler was Suleiman the Magnificent. He ruled from 1520 to 1566. He fought battles but also wrote laws to keep the peace.

Istanbul

Plate

ANATOLIA

Izmir

GREECE

Ottoman craft workers made ceramics decorated with flowers.

CRETE

CYPRUS

SYRIA

MEDITERRANEAN SEA

Damascus

Baghdad

Jerusalem

Cairo

Bedouins with camels

PERSIAN GULF

Woman wearing veil
The women of the Ottoman Empire covered their heads or faces with veils.

Traveling Arabs, called Bedouins, crossed the desert with their camels carrying goods to sell.

EGYPT

RED SEA

Mecca

Coastal empire
The Ottoman Empire stretched along the coasts of Europe, North Africa, and the Middle East. It included many cultures.

SCALE

0   250 miles

0   250 kilometers

53

The Renaissance

Beginning in the 1400s, there were big advances in art and science in Europe. Artists were inspired by ancient Greek and Roman works of art, which had been rediscovered. That is why this period is called the Renaissance, meaning "rebirth." New ideas were spread quickly thanks to the invention of the printing press in Germany.

SCOTLAND

Martin Luther defending his ideas in 1521

Erasmus was a famous Renaissance writer and thinker.

In England, composers wrote music for the lute, a stringed instrument.

 **Lute**

Erasmus

ENGLAND

London

Antwerp

Ghent

The church divides

In 1517 Martin Luther, a German priest, challenged many of the teachings of the Catholic Church. As a result, Luther's followers founded new Protestant churches.

Paris

ATLANTIC OCEAN

FRANCE

New view of Earth

The church taught that Earth was the center of the universe. But in the early 1500s, the Polish astronomer Nicolas Copernicus argued that Earth and the other planets moved around the sun.

Model universe with Earth at the center

The astrolabe was used by Portuguese explorers to find their way at sea.

*In the **1400s**, Portuguese ships set off to explore the coast of Africa.*

Astrolabe

Madrid

SPAIN

 Lisbon

Portuguese ship

PORTUGAL

NORWAY

Stockholm

N
W E
S

SWEDEN

BALTIC SEA

DENMARK

Copenhagen

Jan van Eyck
Northern Renaissance artists, like Jan van Eyck from the Netherlands, painted in a new, lifelike style. This portrait of a married couple skillfully uses light to make things look realistic.

Arnolfini portrait, 1434

HOLY ROMAN EMPIRE

Wittenberg

Dürer was an influential German painter and printmaker.

Dürer

Michelangelo's *David*
Ancient Greek sculpture inspired the Italian artist Michelangelo to create beautiful new works of art. In the early 1500s, he carved a famous statue of David, a hero from the Bible.

Mainz

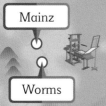

Worms

Nuremberg

HUNGARY

Venice in Italy was the most important trading port in Europe.

Venice

Genoa

Trading ship

Florence

Florence Cathedral

In 1436, Filippo Brunelleschi built a huge dome for Florence Cathedral, inspired by an ancient Roman dome.

OTTOMAN EMPIRE

Rome

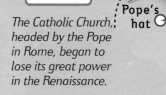

The Catholic Church, headed by the Pope in Rome, began to lose its great power in the Renaissance.

Pope's hat

Naples

ITALY

Connected continent
Much of Europe is close to the sea and linked by rivers. This meant new ideas could spread either by water or land.

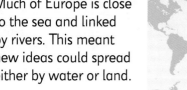

SCALE

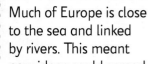

0   200 miles

0   200 kilometers

MEDITERRANEAN SEA

Slave ship
The voyage across the Atlantic was called the Middle Passage. Slaves were kept chained below deck, crammed together so the ship could carry as many people as possible.

UNITED STATES OF AMERICA

Ships sailed to the United States with African slaves to be sold in markets.

Slaves picking cotton

Slaves were forced to pick cotton without being paid.

Slaves

Ships sailed from the Caribbean to Europe with sugar and rum.

MEXICO

CUBA

JAMAICA

HAITI

Sugar and rum

Slave market
In the Americas, slaves were sold at public auctions in port towns. They could be bought and sold again by many different owners.

SURINAME

Slaves worked in gold, silver, and diamond mines in Brazil.

PERU

Gold mines

Diamond mines

Silver mines

BRAZIL

The slave trade

Slaves are people treated as property and forced to do work. Slavery was carried out on a huge scale after Europeans settled in the Americas. From the 16th to the 19th centuries, Europeans took 12 million African slaves across the Atlantic. In North America, slaves worked on big farms called plantations.

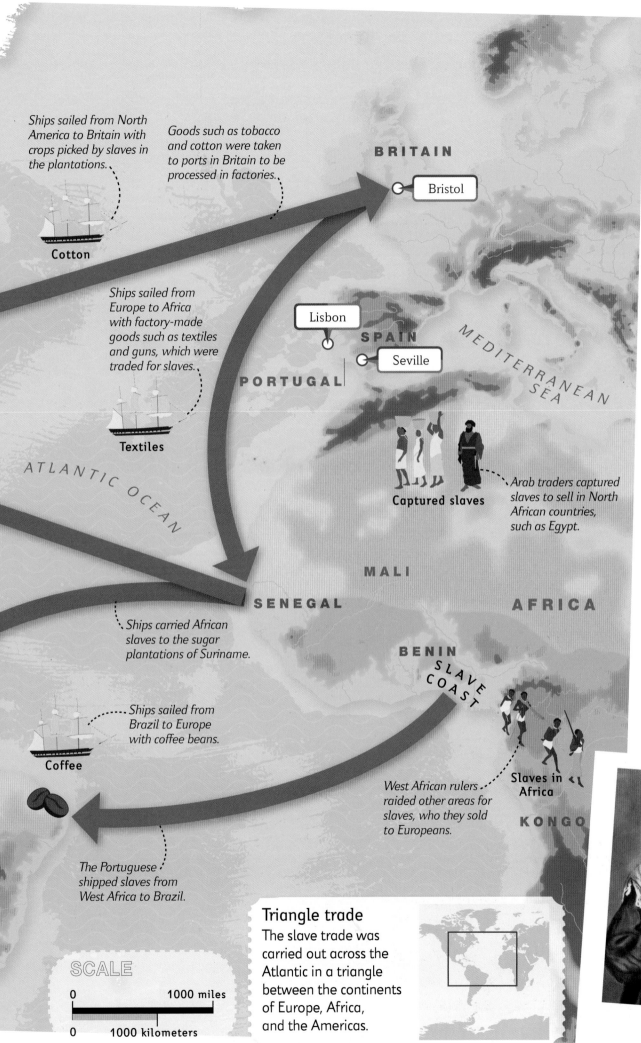

Trade route
Slaves and goods were moved on these routes.

Cotton
Fibers of cotton can be woven into cloth.

Tobacco
Dried tobacco leaves for smoking.

Cocoa
The cocoa bean is used to make chocolate.

Coffee
Coffee beans are used to make the hot drink.

Sugar
Sugar was shipped in shapes called loaves.

Ships
Sailing ships carried people and goods across the Atlantic.

Ships sailed from North America to Britain with crops picked by slaves in the plantations.

Goods such as tobacco and cotton were taken to ports in Britain to be processed in factories.

BRITAIN

Bristol

Ships sailed from Europe to Africa with factory-made goods such as textiles and guns, which were traded for slaves.

Lisbon

SPAIN

Seville

PORTUGAL

MEDITERRANEAN SEA

Cotton

Textiles

ATLANTIC OCEAN

Captured slaves

Arab traders captured slaves to sell in North African countries, such as Egypt.

MALI

AFRICA

SENEGAL

Ships carried African slaves to the sugar plantations of Suriname.

BENIN

SLAVE COAST

Ships sailed from Brazil to Europe with coffee beans.

Coffee

West African rulers raided other areas for slaves, who they sold to Europeans.

Slaves in Africa

KONGO

The Portuguese shipped slaves from West Africa to Brazil.

Ending slavery

Abolitionists like Sojourner Truth, a former slave, were people who campaigned to end slavery. Britain banned the selling of slaves in 1807, but slavery continued in the Americas until the late 19th century.

Triangle trade

The slave trade was carried out across the Atlantic in a triangle between the continents of Europe, Africa, and the Americas.

SCALE

0 — 1000 miles

0 — 1000 kilometers

Sojourner Truth

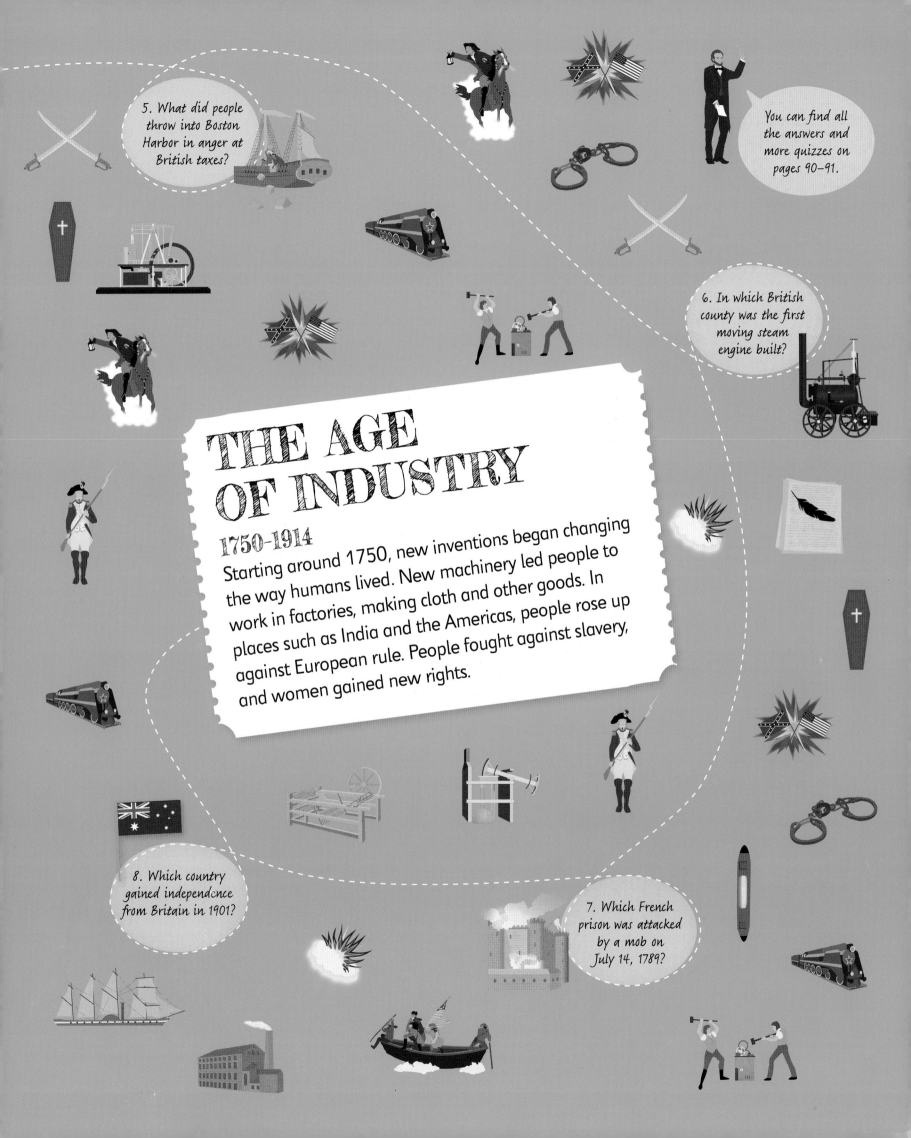

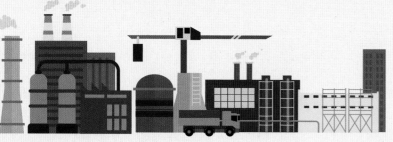

The age of industry

Starting around 1750, the world began to change very quickly. People rose up against their rulers, and many countries became independent for the first time. The invention of steam power led to new ways of making things and getting around. This Industrial Revolution completely changed how people lived and worked.

1756–1763
Seven Years' War
At the end of this war, the British Empire grows. It takes land from the French Empire in Canada, America, and India.

1770
James Cook
James Cook makes maps of the eastern coast of Australia, then claims Australia for Britain.

James Cook

Aboriginal warrior

1790
Australian revolt
Native Australian people called aborigines begin to fight back against the newly arrived British.

1791–1804
Haitian revolution
Slave workers on plantations in Haiti revolt, led by Toussaint Louverture. Haiti becomes the first black-ruled state in the Americas.

1800–1815
Napoleonic Wars
The French ruler, Napoleon, tries to conquer other countries in Europe and fights wars against other European nations.

1856
Steel
Henry Bessemer invents a process to create steel that is strong enough to make railroads, skyscrapers, and machines.

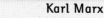

1848
Communist Manifesto
Karl Marx and Friedrich Engels write and publish *The Communist Manifesto*, describing their radical new ideas about how money should be divided between people.

Karl Marx

1839–1842
First Opium War
Britain starts a war against China to force China to trade. In 1842, Britain wins the war and takes Hong Kong.

1857–1858
Indian Mutiny
India tries to become independent from British rule but does not succeed.

1861–1865
American Civil War
In the United States, North and South go to war over slavery. The North wins and slavery is abolished.

1867
Canadian independence
Canada becomes an independent country and is no longer ruled by Great Britain.

1868
Meiji Restoration
Emperor Meiji takes control of Japan and modernizes how the country is ruled.

Emperor Meiji

1914
Outbreak of World War 1
Archduke Franz Ferdinand is shot, which triggers a series of events leading to World War I.

1913
Ottoman retreat
The Ottoman Empire loses the First Balkan War, and most of its lands in Europe.

1912
Chinese Revolution
Sun Yat-sen leads a revolution in China, overthrowing the Manchu dynasty, which had ruled for 276 years.

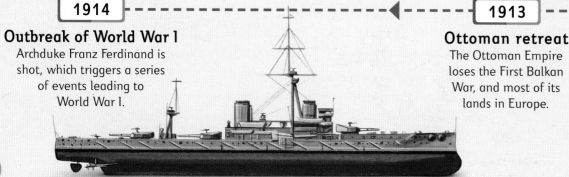

Warship

1770
Slave trade
The slave trade reached its peak in the 18th century, with 80,000 slaves brought from West Africa to America every year.

1771
First modern factory
Richard Arkwright builds the water frame, a spinning machine that is powered by water wheels. His invention is quickly copied.

1775–1783
US independence
The United States approves the Declaration of Independence on July 4, 1776, breaking free from Britain. The new nation is made of 13 colonies.

Early steam engine

1789–1799
French Revolution
People in Paris rebel. They overthrow their king and queen.

Vive La France!

1776
Steam engine
James Watt develops the first of his many steam engines and introduces the term "horsepower" to show how powerful his engines are.

Napoleon

1803
Denmark bans slavery
Denmark is the first European country to ban slavery.

1811–1828
Independent Americas
Several American countries fight wars against their Spanish rulers, winning independence.

1821–1832
Greek War of Independence
Greece becomes independent, winning its freedom from the Ottoman Empire.

1831
First electrical motor
Michael Faraday, a British physicist and chemist, invents the first electric motor.

1829
Prize-winning steam engine
George Stephenson designs the *Rocket*, which wins a competition to power the Liverpool & Manchester Railway.

Stephenson's *Rocket*

1822
Brazilian independence
Brazil wins its independence from Portugal. Pedro I becomes the founder and first ruler of the empire of Brazil.

First telephone

1876
Telephone invented
Alexander Graham Bell invents the first telephone. People are able to talk over long distances for the first time.

1876
Internal combustion engine invented
Nikolaus Otto invents the combustion engine, which can be used to power cars, trucks, and motorcycles.

1893
Votes for women
New Zealand is the first country to give women equal voting rights. The next country to do so will be Australia, in 1903.

1904–1905
Russo-Japanese War
Japan defeats Russia with clever new tactics and weapons. Japan is seen as a world power for the first time.

Communism grew in Russia after the Russo-Japanese War

1903
First airplane
The Wright brothers successfully fly the first powered airplane.

Australian flag

1901
Australian independence
Australia becomes independent and is no longer under British rule.

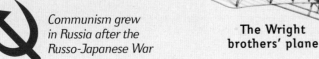

The Wright brothers' plane

American Revolution

Before the United States was a country, there were 13 British colonies in America. In 1775, they rose up against the British because they wanted to rule themselves. This type of change in government is called a revolution. The colonies fought many battles with the British. In 1783, peace was made, and the United States of America ecame an independent country.

American war

The fighting took place along the East Coast of North America. Most of the battles were clustered in the same areas.

SCALE

0   100 miles

0   100 kilometers

New flag

On June 14, 1777, the Americans flew a new flag. The 13 stars and 13 stripes represented the 13 colonies. Since then, a new star has been added for each new state. There are now 50.

At midnight on April 18, 1775, Paul Revere rode out to warn people that British troops were coming.

MASSACHUSETTS

NEW HAMPSHIRE

Midnight ride

Boston Tea Party

The colonists won two battles at Saratoga, gaining them support from the French, Dutch, and Spanish.

Saratoga October 17, 1777

NEW YORK

MASSACHUSETTS

Boston

In anger at British taxes on tea sold in America, colonists threw tea into Boston Harbor on December 16, 1773.

RHODE ISLAND

CONNETICUT

New York

Approved on July 4, 1776, this document rejected British rule.

PENNSYLVANIA

Philadelphia

MARYLAND

Declaration of Independence

NEW JERSEY

On December 25, 1776, Washington's army crossed the Delaware to surprise and defeat British troops at Trenton.

Delaware river crossing

ATLANTIC OCEAN

The British were defeated at the battle of Yorktown. They surrendered, ending the war.

VIRGINIA

DELAWARE

Yorktown October 19, 1781

Yorktown

KEY

⚔ Important battles
Key fights between the Americans and the British.

NORTH CAROLINA

SOUTH CAROLINA

Camden January 16, 1781

GEORGIA

Charleston June 28, 1776

George Washington

A former farmer, Washington (1732–1799) became leader of the American army in 1775. After the war, he helped set up the new US government and became the first US president in 1789.

George Washington, in 1795

Palace of Versailles

Louis XVI lived in splendor in the huge Palace of Versailles, near Paris. In October 1789, thousands of starving women marched from Paris to Versailles because bread prices were too high.

European revolution

France is in Europe. At the time of the revolution, it was surrounded by countries still ruled by kings and queens.

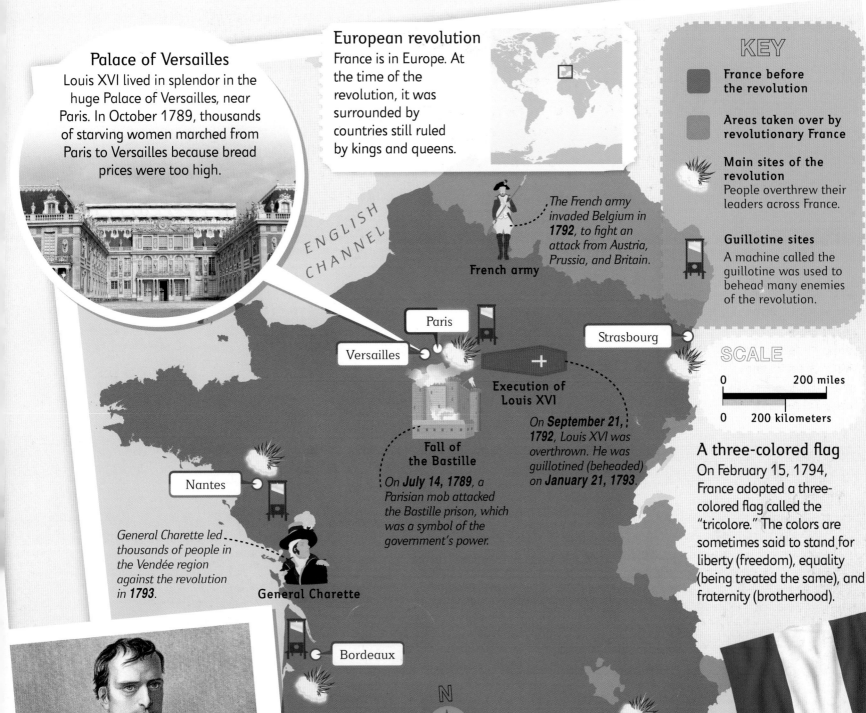

ENGLISH CHANNEL

The French army invaded Belgium in **1792**, to fight an attack from Austria, Prussia, and Britain.

French army

Paris

Versailles

Strasbourg

Execution of Louis XVI

On **September 21, 1792**, Louis XVI was overthrown. He was guillotined (beheaded) on **January 21, 1793**.

Fall of the Bastille

On **July 14, 1789**, a Parisian mob attacked the Bastille prison, which was a symbol of the government's power.

Nantes

General Charette led thousands of people in the Vendée region against the revolution in **1793**.

General Charette

Bordeaux

N W E S

Marseille

A three-colored flag

On February 15, 1794, France adopted a three-colored flag called the "tricolore." The colors are sometimes said to stand for liberty (freedom), equality (being treated the same), and fraternity (brotherhood).

Napoleon Bonaparte, in the 1800s

Napoleon Bonaparte

In 1799, a brilliant French army general called Napoleon (1769–1821) overthrew the new government. He crowned himself emperor of France in 1804. Napoleon conquered most of Europe, before being defeated by Britain and Prussia in 1815.

French Revolution

In 1789, many people in France were starving. They rose up against their king, Louis XVI, and his government. In 1792, the French people set up a republic, which meant they could choose how France was ruled. King Louis and thousands of his supporters were killed.

The Industrial Revolution

Britain changed a lot in the 18th century. New machines were invented, and modern factories opened for the first time, making cloth and other goods in huge amounts. People moved from the countryside to perform factory work in smoky new towns. This period was called the Industrial Revolution.

Industrial towns

New towns sprang up across Britain, housing thousands of workers. Many houses were built back-to-back, with no outside space. Diseases spread quickly in the cramped streets, and living conditions were very bad.

Newcastle upon Tyne, 1877

Cotton-factory workers

Factories

Factories were built to contain new machines. Many of the factories made cloth. People who used to make cloth in their own homes now worked long hours inside busy, noisy factories instead.

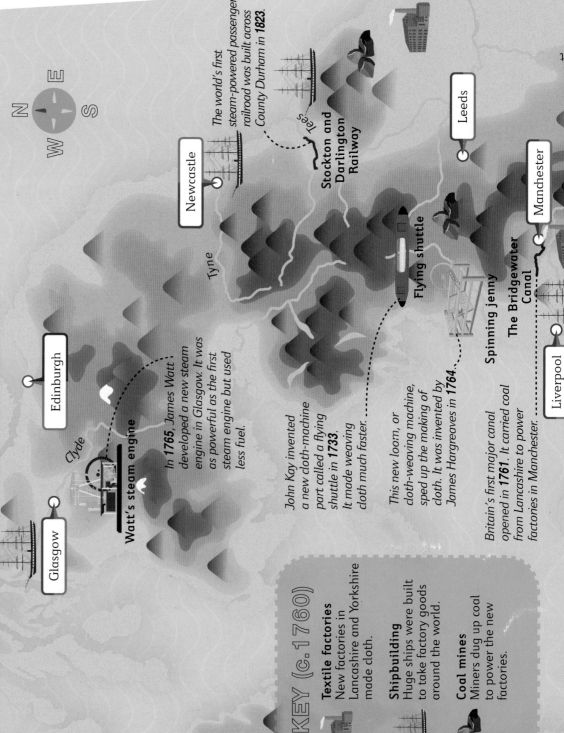

Glasgow

Edinburgh

In 1765, James Watt developed a new steam engine in Glasgow. It was as powerful as the first steam engine but used less fuel.

Watt's steam engine

Clyde

Newcastle

Tyne

Tees

The world's first steam-powered passenger railroad was built across County Durham in 1823.

Stockton and Darlington Railway

Flying shuttle

John Kay invented a new cloth-machine part called a flying shuttle in 1733. It made weaving cloth much faster.

This new loom, or cloth-weaving machine, sped up the making of cloth. It was invented by James Hargreaves in 1764.

Spinning jenny

The Bridgewater Canal

Britain's first major canal opened in 1761. It carried coal from Lancashire to power factories in Manchester.

Leeds

Manchester

Liverpool

KEY (c. 1760)

Textile factories
New factories in Lancashire and Yorkshire made cloth.

Shipbuilding
Huge ships were built to take factory goods around the world.

Coal mines
Miners dug up coal to power the new factories.

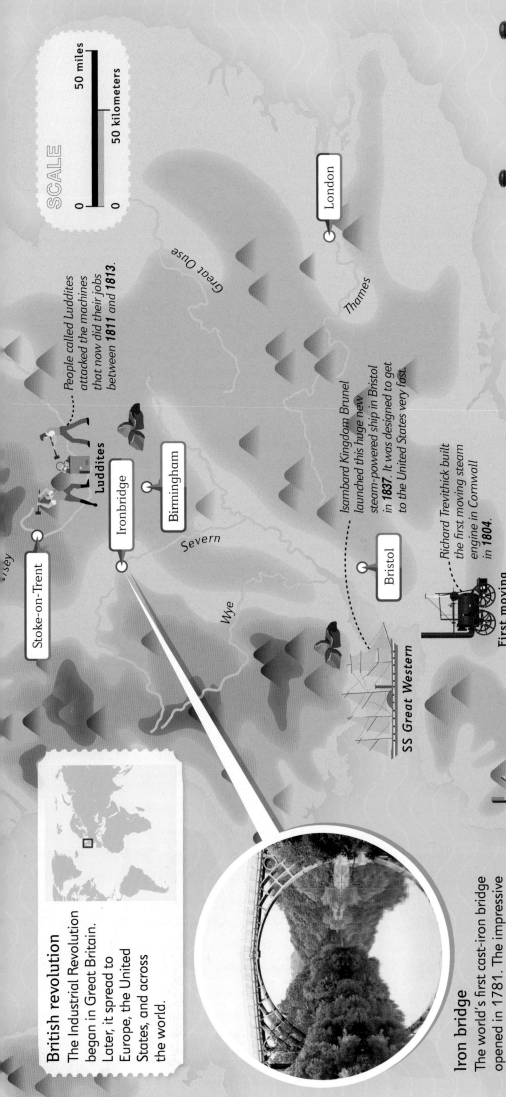

50 miles
0
0   50 kilometers

British revolution

The Industrial Revolution began in Great Britain. Later, it spread to Europe, the United States, and across the world.

Great Ouse

London

Thames

*People called Luddites attacked the machines that now did their jobs between **1811** and **1813**.*

Luddites

Stoke-on-Trent

Ironbridge

Birmingham

Severn

Wye

*Isambard Kingdom Brunel launched this huge new steam-powered ship in Bristol in **1837**. It was designed to get to the United States very fast.*

Bristol

*Richard Trevithick built the first moving steam engine in Cornwall in **1804**.*

First moving steam engine

*In **1712**, Thomas Newcomen built the first steam engine. It pumped water out of mines.*

SS Great Western

First steam engine

ENGLISH CHANNEL

Iron bridge

The world's first cast-iron bridge opened in 1781. The impressive structure crosses the River Severn in Shropshire, in an industrial area now known as Ironbridge.

Cotton-spinning frame

New inventions

There were many new inventions in the Industrial Revolution. New machines and high-powered steam engines made it faster to create products, such as cotton and wool cloth, iron tools, machines, and pottery.

Child labor

Children as young as four worked in the new factories and coal mines. Their work was often dangerous, and many were killed. Laws were passed from the 1830s onward to limit the hours and ages at which children were allowed to work.

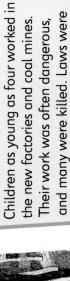

A child textile-factory worker

65

The Civil War

In 1861, a war broke out in the United States that split the country in two. Eleven states feared that the government would free African-American slaves, workers who were owned by other people and not paid. These states left, or seceded from, the United States to form the Confederacy. The states that remained loyal to the United States were known as the Union. The two sides fought for four years.

Abraham Lincoln in 1860

The Confederate flag

When the 11 Southern states left the Union and set up the Confederacy, they created their own flag. The 13 stars stood for the Confederate states and the states that supported them.

The Confederate flag

President Lincoln

Abraham Lincoln was elected president of the United States in November 1860. He spoke out against slavery, causing 11 southern states to leave the Union. Lincoln led the Union to victory in 1865.

ILL

KANSAS

MISSOURI

KEY (1861)

Union states
Twenty-three states remained in the Union.

Confederate states
Eleven slave-owning states left the Union to join the Confederacy.

Slave-owning Union states
Some states stayed in the Union but allowed slavery.

Other territories
These territories did not get involved in the war.

 Cotton fields
Slaves grew cotton on plantations in the South.

 Union ships
These blocked other ships from getting into and out of the South. This made it hard to buy and sell things in the Confederacy.

 Conflicts
Places where the Union and Confederate armies fought.

OKLAHOMA

ARKANSAS

MISSI

TEXAS

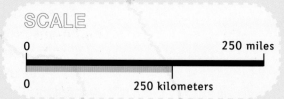

SCALE

0 ———————————— 250 miles

0 ———————————— 250 kilometers

After a long battle, the Confederate fort of Vicksburg surrendered on *July 4, 1863*. Its surrender cut the Confederacy in two.

Siege of Vicksburg

Divided country

The Civil War was fought between the Southern Confederate and the Northern Union states of the United States.

LOUISIANA

GULF OF MEXICO

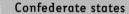

MICHIGAN

LAKE MICHIGAN

NEW YORK

OHIO

INDIANA

NOIS

NEW JERSEY

The Gettysburg Address

In his speech on **November 19, 1863**, President Lincoln called the Civil War a struggle for all people to be treated the same way.

PENNSYLVANIA

Assassination of President Lincoln

On **April 14, 1865**, Lincoln was shot by slavery-supporter John Wilkes Booth. He died the next day.

MARYLAND

Washington DC

WEST VIRGINIA

First Battle of Bull Run

The first major battle of the war was fought on **July 21, 1861**. Union troops failed to seize an important railroad junction.

Richmond

KENTUCKY

VIRGINIA

Siege of Petersburg

Union troops won the Confederate towns of Richmond and Petersburg between **June 9, 1864** and **March 25, 1865**.

General Lee

General Robert E. Lee surrendered on behalf of the Confederates, ending the war on **April 9, 1865**.

TENNESSEE

NORTH CAROLINA

Union troops won this big battle on **April 7, 1862**. An important Confederate general, Albert Johnson, died in the fight.

Battle of Shiloh

The war was started by a Confederate attack on Fort Sumter in Charleston, South Carolina, **April 12, 1863**.

SOUTH CAROLINA

ALABAMA

Capture of Atlanta

GEORGIA

Fort Sumter, Charleston

ATLANTIC OCEAN

SIPPI

Union general William Sherman seized Atlanta, an important railroad hub, on **September 2, 1864**. His troops set parts of the city on fire.

General Sherman's Union army destroyed buildings on its way to the coast between **November 15** and **December 21, 1864**.

March to the Sea

The Emancipation Proclamation

On January 1, 1863, President Lincoln ordered all slaves in the Confederacy to be freed. In 1865, the 13th Amendment to the US Constitution freed every slave in the Union.

FLORIDA

Newly freed slaves

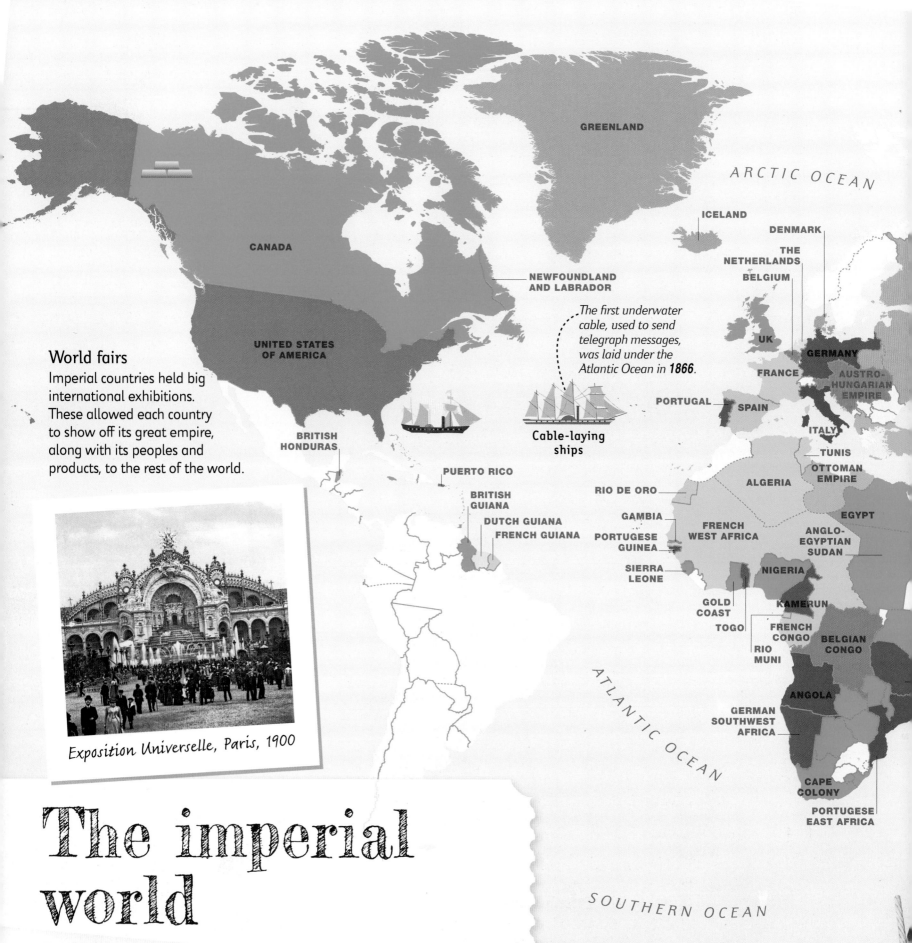

ARCTIC OCEAN

GREENLAND

ICELAND

DENMARK

THE NETHERLANDS

BELGIUM

CANADA

NEWFOUNDLAND AND LABRADOR

UK

GERMANY

FRANCE

AUSTRO-HUNGARIAN EMPIRE

The first underwater cable, used to send telegraph messages, was laid under the Atlantic Ocean in 1866.

PORTUGAL

SPAIN

ITALY

UNITED STATES OF AMERICA

Cable-laying ships

TUNIS

OTTOMAN EMPIRE

World fairs

Imperial countries held big international exhibitions. These allowed each country to show off its great empire, along with its peoples and products, to the rest of the world.

BRITISH HONDURAS

PUERTO RICO

BRITISH GUIANA

DUTCH GUIANA

FRENCH GUIANA

RIO DE ORO

ALGERIA

EGYPT

GAMBIA

PORTUGESE GUINEA

FRENCH WEST AFRICA

ANGLO-EGYPTIAN SUDAN

SIERRA LEONE

NIGERIA

GOLD COAST

TOGO

KAMERUN

FRENCH CONGO

RIO MUNI

BELGIAN CONGO

ANGOLA

Exposition Universelle, Paris, 1900

GERMAN SOUTHWEST AFRICA

ATLANTIC OCEAN

CAPE COLONY

PORTUGESE EAST AFRICA

The imperial world

SOUTHERN OCEAN

By 1900, most of the world was controlled by a few European nations. The part of the world ruled by each nation was called its empire. Europeans called the foreign countries they ruled their colonies.

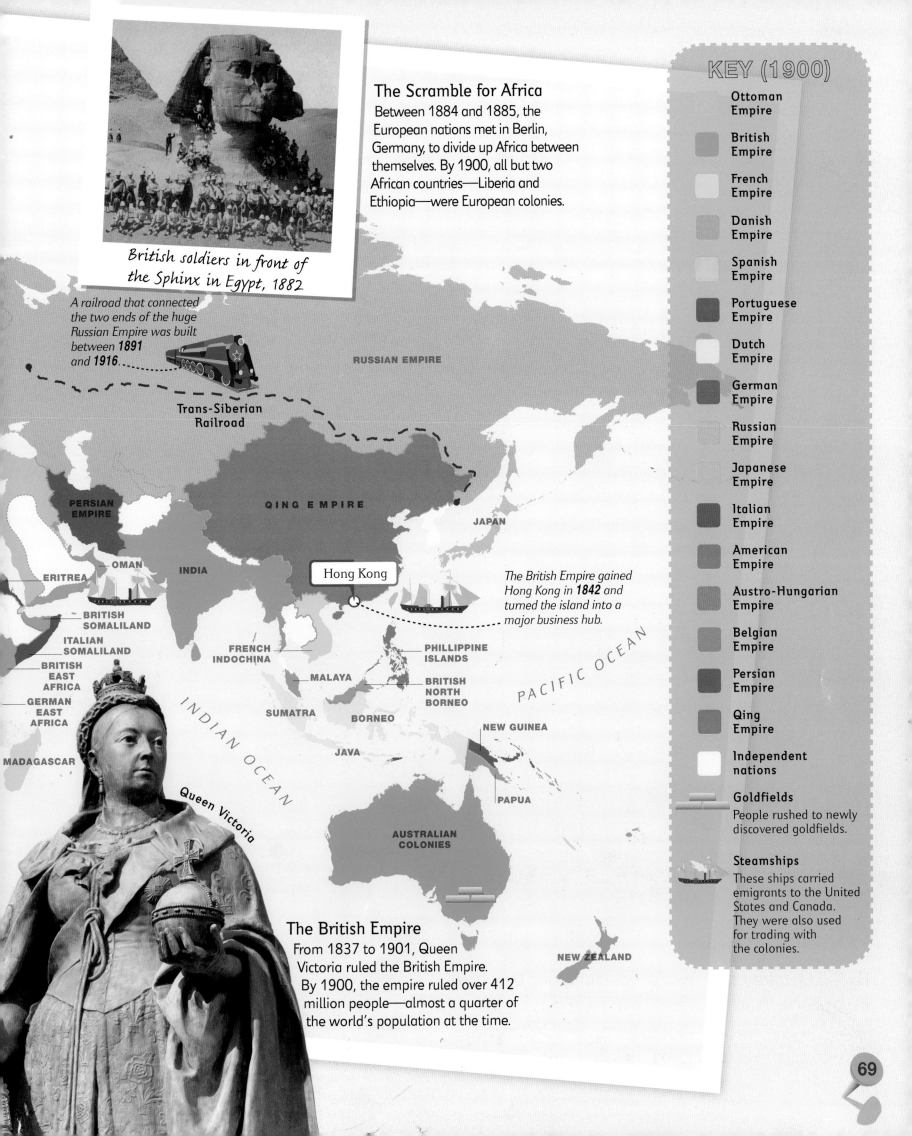

The Scramble for Africa

Between 1884 and 1885, the European nations met in Berlin, Germany, to divide up Africa between themselves. By 1900, all but two African countries—Liberia and Ethiopia—were European colonies.

British soldiers in front of the Sphinx in Egypt, 1882

A railroad that connected the two ends of the huge Russian Empire was built between 1891 and 1916.

Trans-Siberian Railroad

RUSSIAN EMPIRE

PERSIAN EMPIRE

QING EMPIRE

JAPAN

Hong Kong

The British Empire gained Hong Kong in 1842 and turned the island into a major business hub.

ERITREA

OMAN

INDIA

BRITISH SOMALILAND

ITALIAN SOMALILAND

BRITISH EAST AFRICA

GERMAN EAST AFRICA

MADAGASCAR

FRENCH INDOCHINA

MALAYA

SUMATRA

BORNEO

JAVA

PHILLIPPINE ISLANDS

BRITISH NORTH BORNEO

NEW GUINEA

PAPUA

INDIAN OCEAN

PACIFIC OCEAN

Queen Victoria

AUSTRALIAN COLONIES

NEW ZEALAND

The British Empire

From 1837 to 1901, Queen Victoria ruled the British Empire. By 1900, the empire ruled over 412 million people—almost a quarter of the world's population at the time.

KEY (1900)

- Ottoman Empire
- British Empire
- French Empire
- Danish Empire
- Spanish Empire
- Portuguese Empire
- Dutch Empire
- German Empire
- Russian Empire
- Japanese Empire
- Italian Empire
- American Empire
- Austro-Hungarian Empire
- Belgian Empire
- Persian Empire
- Qing Empire
- Independent nations

Goldfields
People rushed to newly discovered goldfields.

Steamships
These ships carried emigrants to the United States and Canada. They were also used for trading with the colonies.

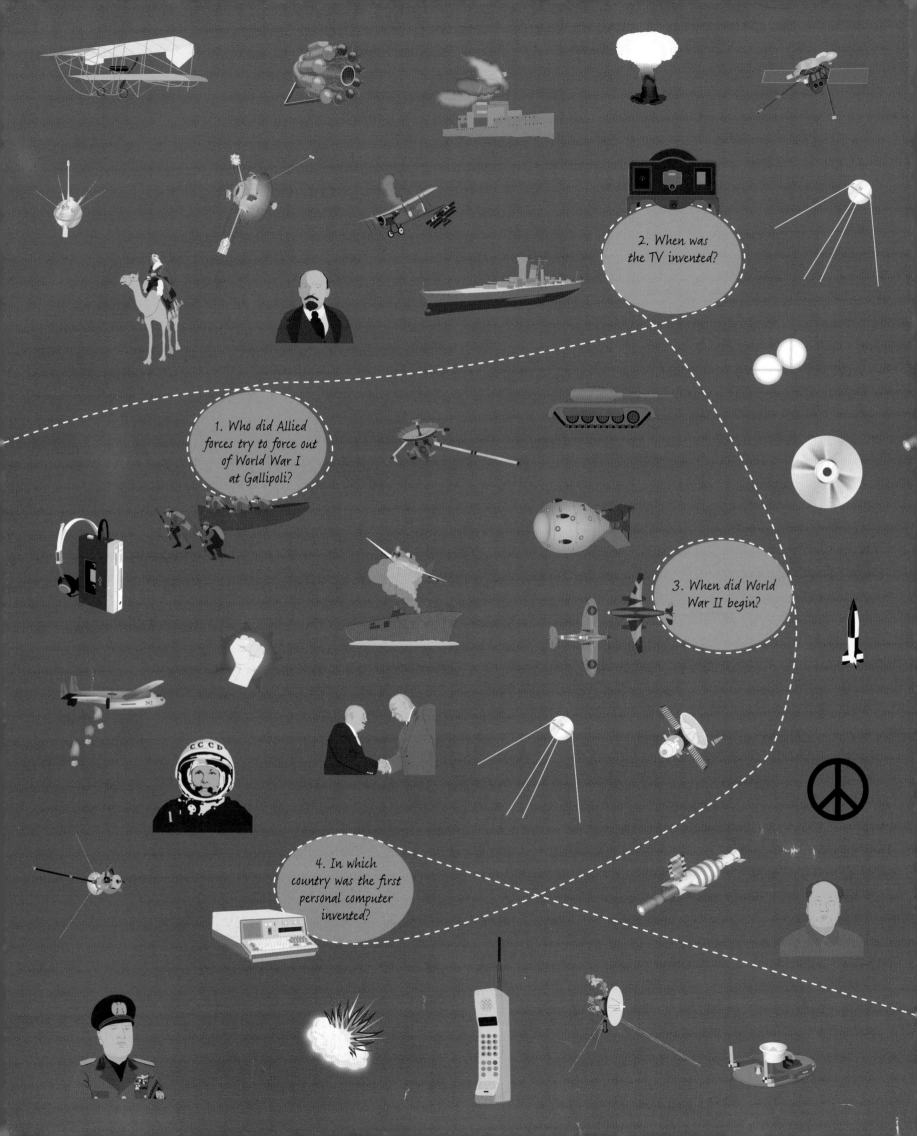

6. When did the Berlin Wall fall?

7. What is the world's newest nation?

THE MODERN WORLD

1914-now

Between 1914 and today, the world has seen some of the deadliest wars in history. People have continued to fight their governments to bring about change. Humans have also been to space for the first time and invented amazing new technology.

You can find all the answers and more quizzes on pages 90-91.

5. Which country was Mussolini leader of?

The modern world

The world today has been shaped by two world wars, huge political changes, and amazing new inventions. People have fought to create many different types of government. The population continues to grow, and exciting new technology is still being developed.

1914–1918
World War 1
A war that begins in Europe in 1914 is fought around the world for four years. More than 18 million people are killed.

Gas mask used in WWI

1917
Russia in revolt
Russia gets rid of its tsar (king) and becomes the first communist country, aiming for everyone to be equal.

1939–1945
World War II
The biggest war in human history breaks out in Europe in 1939 and soon spreads around the world. More than 60 million people are killed.

1936–1939
Spanish Civil War
The Spanish Army led by General Franco fights against the elected government, winning power over the whole of Spain in 1939.

WWII fighter plane

1957
Ghana gains independence
The Gold Coast becomes the first black, British-ruled colony in Africa to gain independence, becoming the country of Ghana.

Flag of Ghana

1957
EEC founded
Six European nations form the European Economic Community (EEC), making it easier for them to trade (buy and sell) goods with each other.

1953
Everest is conquered
New Zealander Edmund Hillary and Tenzing Norgay from Nepal become the first people to climb Everest, the world's highest mountain.

1957
Sputnik 1 flies around the world
The USSR launches the first satellite made by humans into space. It takes 96.2 minutes to orbit (travel around) Earth.

1961
JFK becomes US president
At 43, John F. Kennedy becomes the youngest president in US history. He is shot dead in 1963.

John F. Kennedy on a half-dollar coin

1962
Cuban missile crisis
The United States and the USSR almost go to war after the USSR places nuclear missiles on the island of Cuba, close to the United States.

1964–1975
Vietnam War
The United States fights with South Vietnam against communist North Vietnam. In 1975, North Vietnam wins control of all Vietnam.

2016
Britain votes to leave the EU
A member of the EU since 1973, Britain votes to leave the group.

EU Flag

2012
World population above 7 billion
The total population of the world rises above 7 billion for the first time.

2002
The Euro
Twelve members of a group of countries in Europe called the European Union (EU) begin using the same money—the Euro.

Euro bill and coins

2001
9/11
Islamic terrorist group al-Qaeda flies two planes into the Twin Towers in New York City. Almost 3,000 people are killed.

1925
Black-and-white TV developed
Scottish engineer John Logie Baird makes the first working black-and-white TV. Color TV follows in 1928.

Early TV

1928
Penicillin
Scottish scientist Alexander Fleming discovers a new medicine called penicillin. It is used to cure infections and saves many lives.

1929
Great Depression
There is an economic slump from 1929–1939, which means people around the world lose their jobs and don't have enough money.

1933
Nazis come to power
Adolf Hitler's Nazi Party comes to power in Germany. The Nazis soon ban all other political parties—only the Nazi Party is allowed to exist.

Nazi badge

1932
Roosevelt elected US president
Franklin Roosevelt wins the presidency and promises to create more jobs so that people can earn money.

President Roosevelt

1946
First electronic computer
ENIAC, the world's first electronic computer, is built in the United States. It is nicknamed "Great Brain."

Flag of India

1947
India and Pakistan become independent
The British give up rule in India. India and Pakistan become independent. Ceylon (Sri Lanka) and Burma (Myanmar) become independent in 1948.

Flag of Pakistan

1950–1953
Korean War
A war breaks out in Korea as North Korea seeks to take over South Korea. The United States fights alongside South Korea.

Tank used in Korean war

1949
China becomes communist
After a lengthy civil war, the Communist Party led by Chairman Mao Zedong takes power in China.

1948
Israel is founded
A new state for Jews is created in the Middle East. Fighting with the Palestinians who already lived in the area turns into a war between Israel and neighboring countries.

1969
Moon landing
American astronaut Neil Armstrong becomes the first person to walk on the moon.

1973
First PC designed
The world's first personal computer (PC) is designed and developed by IBM in California. It is much smaller than earlier computers.

1982
CDs introduced
Technology companies Philips and Sony produce the first compact disc (CD), to store data such as music.

CDs

1994
Apartheid ends
South Africa ends its policy of apartheid, which treated white and black people differently. Nelson Mandela becomes the new president.

Statue of Nelson Mandela celebrating freedom

1991
USSR breaks up
The Cold War between anti-communist and communist countries ends when the communist USSR collapses. New states are created, including Russia.

1989
Berlin Wall falls
As communism ends in Eastern Europe, the Berlin Wall dividing West Berlin and communist East Berlin is pulled down. The city is reunited after 44 years apart.

Inventions

The 20th century was a period of great technological change. The world's first airplane, first rocket, and first satellite were all in the sky by 1957. Toward the beginning of the 21st century, computers and cell phones transformed the world. Today, new inventions continue to improve human life.

UNIVAC, an early computer

The computer revolution
The first computers, created in the 1940s, were huge machines that worked slowly. Today's computers are small, fast, and can do many different things. Modern computers have changed the way we work, live, learn, and entertain ourselves.

NORTH AMERICA

Martin Cooper developed the world's first cell phone in 1973. It was about the size of a brick.

First handheld cell phone

The world's first personal computer was designed and developed by IBM in California in 1973.

First personal computer

First electronic computer

ENIAC, the world's first electronic computer, was built in Pennsylvania in 1946.

First integrated circuit (microchip)

In 1958, Jack Kilby created a tiny electronic circuit called a microchip. This changed the way technology was powered.

PACIFIC OCEAN

SOUTH AMERICA

ATLANTIC OCEAN

Taking to the skies
Orville Wright was the first person to make a powered flight, above North Carolina in 1903. Thanks to the development of powerful gas engines, he flew 120 feet (37 m) in 12 seconds on board the *Flyer*.

The Wright Flyer

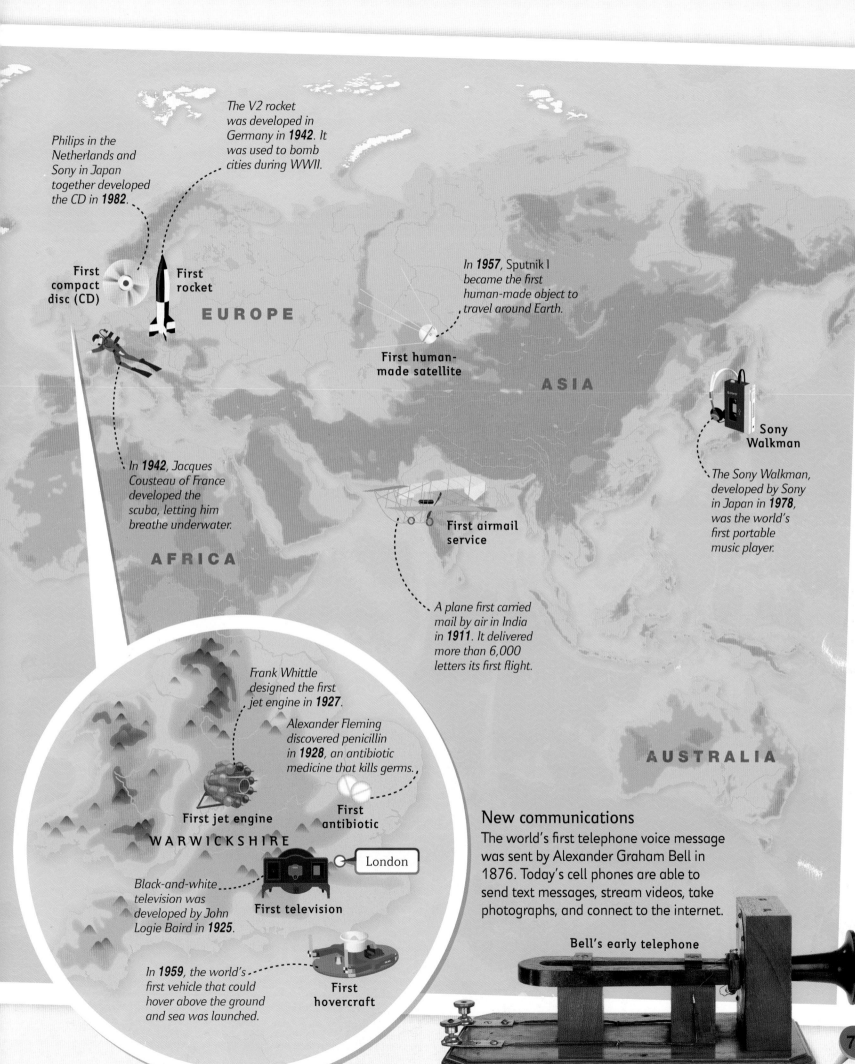

Philips in the Netherlands and Sony in Japan together developed the CD in *1982*.

First compact disc (CD)

The V2 rocket was developed in Germany in *1942*. It was used to bomb cities during WWII.

First rocket

EUROPE

In *1957*, Sputnik I became the first human-made object to travel around Earth.

First human-made satellite

ASIA

In *1942*, Jacques Cousteau of France developed the scuba, letting him breathe underwater.

AFRICA

Sony Walkman

The Sony Walkman, developed by Sony in Japan in *1978*, was the world's first portable music player.

First airmail service

A plane first carried mail by air in India in *1911*. It delivered more than 6,000 letters its first flight.

Frank Whittle designed the first jet engine in *1927*.

Alexander Fleming discovered penicillin in *1928*, an antibiotic medicine that kills germs.

First jet engine

First antibiotic

WARWICKSHIRE

London

AUSTRALIA

Black-and-white television was developed by John Logie Baird in *1925*.

First television

New communications
The world's first telephone voice message was sent by Alexander Graham Bell in 1876. Today's cell phones are able to send text messages, stream videos, take photographs, and connect to the internet.

In *1959*, the world's first vehicle that could hover above the ground and sea was launched.

First hovercraft

Bell's early telephone

World War I

In June 1914, a war began in Europe that grew to become the First World War. The Central Powers, led by Germany, fought the Allies—Britain, France, Russia, and, eventually, the United States. Millions of soldiers were killed in deadly battles on land and at sea. The Allies won the war in November 1918.

Franz Ferdinand in 1914

War begins

Austria-Hungary declared war on Serbia after a Serb shot an Austrian prince, Franz Ferdinand, in June 1914. European countries joined the two sides, and war broke out across Europe in August 1914.

ATLANTIC OCEAN

PORTUGAL

SPAIN

MOROCCO

WESTERN SAHARA

ALGERIA

Germany and Britain fight to a draw at the war's biggest naval battle in 1916.

Jutland

NORWAY

DENMARK

S

GREAT BRITAIN

NETHERLANDS

German zeppelins (airships) dropped bombs on cities in Britain.

London

GERMANY

Ypres, 1915
Passchendaele, 1917

BELGIUM

The Somme, 1916

Paris

Marne, 1914

Verdun, 1916

Pilots fought "dogfights" high above the battlefields.

Dogfights

LUXEMBOURG

Caporetto, 1917

SWITZERLAND

FRANCE

ITALY

Isonzo, 1915–1917

W N E S

Rome

Western front

The fighting in western Europe turned into a stalemate, which meant neither side could win. Both sides dug trenches to defend the ground they had gained. Soldiers lived in these muddy trenches while being fired on by the enemy.

TUNISIA

LIBYA

SCALE

0 — 250 miles

0 — 250 kilometers

DEN

Two revolutions in Russia in 1917 overthrew the tsar (ruler).

Revolutions in St. Petersburg

Moscow

Russia launched deadly attacks against German and Austro-Hungarian forces on the eastern front in 1916.

Tannenberg, 1914

Brusilov offensive

RUSSIA

AUSTRIA-HUNGARY

MONTENEGRO

ROMANIA

SERBIA   BULGARIA

BLACK SEA

Constantinople

ALBANIA

Gallipoli

Allied forces tried to force the Ottoman Empire out of the war in 1915 at Gallipoli.

THE OTTOMAN EMPIRE

GREECE

MEDITERRANEAN SEA

In 1916, the Arabs rose in revolt against their Ottoman rulers, with help from the British.

Jerusalem

EGYPT

Arab Revolt

KEY

Central Powers
Countries in central Europe joined together.

Allies
Britain, France, and Russia teamed up as allies.

Neutrals
Countries not in the war were called neutral.

Battle sites
Soldiers fought each other across Europe.

Women at war
Women weren't allowed to fight in the war, but they still carried out important jobs. They worked on farms to grow crops and in factories to make explosives and bullets for the troops.

NATIONAL SERVICE
WOMEN'S LAND ARMY

"GOD SPEED THE PLOUGH AND THE WOMAN WHO DRIVES IT"

APPLY FOR ENROLMENT FORMS AT YOUR NEAREST POST OFFICE OR EMPLOYMENT EXCHANGE

The Allied leaders in June 1919

War ends

In late 1918, most of the Central Powers had stopped fighting. Germany fought on with exhausted troops in western Europe. A ceasefire ended the war on November 11, 1918, and a peace agreement was signed in June 1919.

Europe at war

Most of the fighting in World War I happened in Europe, though many other countries were affected. America joined the Allies in 1917.

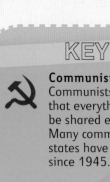
*The fascist Nazi Party ruled Germany from **1933** to **1945**, when they lost World War II.*

**Nazi flag
GERMANY**

**Eastern
Europe
(variou**

*The Spanish Civil War was a conflict between supporters of the fascist General Franco (1892–1975) and believers in democracy. It lasted from **1936** to **1939**.*

**Spanish
Civil War**

**SPAIN
ITALY**

Mussolini

**UNITED STATES
OF AMERICA**

**Anti-nuclear
movement**

Ballot box

People in the United States choose their own government by casting ballots. This is called democracy.

*Benito Mussolini (1883–1945) was the fascist leader of Italy from **1922** to **1943**. He made it illegal to oppose his rule.*

*People began protesting against governments using deadly nuclear weapons in the **1960s**.*

Cuba

ATLANTIC OCEAN

PACIFIC OCEAN

Fascism
Fascists believe in obedience to a powerful leader. The Nazi Party in Germany was a fascist party led by Adolf Hitler (1899–1945). The Nazis believed that Germans were better than all other people.

New ideas

People have often come up with new ideas about society, especially during the early 20th century. Communists believe in rule by a single party, while democrats think that people should have the right to choose their own leaders. Fascists want all-powerful leaders, called dictators. Many people have fought to change the way they are governed.

Adolf Hitler at a Nazi event in 1927

Vladimir Lenin (1870–1924) seized power during the Russian Revolution of 1917 and set up the world's first communist state.

Russia

Joseph Stalin (1878–1953) became leader of communist Russia after 1924 and ruled until his death.

Stalinism

Vladimir Lenin

UNION OF SOVIET SOCIALIST REPUBLICS

Mongolia

North Korea

China

Mao

More than 70 million Chinese people died from famine or execution during Mao Zedong's rule.

INDIA

Laos

Vietnam

Cambodia

INDIAN OCEAN

Green politicians want to protect the environment. The first Green Party was formed in Australia in 1972.

Green politics

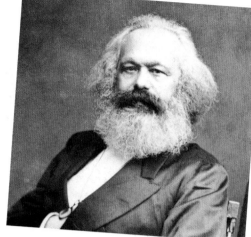

Karl Marx in 1875

Karl Marx

Karl Marx (1818–1883) was a German political thinker. He thought that people could develop a society in which wealth is owned by the whole community rather than by individuals. This is called communism.

Nonviolence

In India, Mahatma Gandhi (1869–1948) wanted to free the country from British rule. He sought to achieve this change through peaceful activities, such as refusing to buy British goods. Gandhi's work helped force the British out of India in 1947.

Communism in China

The Chinese Communist Party's Mao Zedong (1893–1976) won power in 1949 after a war with other political groups in China. He believed in revolution and got rid of his political opponents. Mao's sayings were collected in the *Little Red Book*.

World War II

In 1939, a war broke out in Europe that spread across the world. Bombs were dropped on cities by planes, and millions of soldiers were killed in battle. Both Germany, led by Adolf Hitler and the Nazi Party, and Japan conquered huge empires. They were defeated in 1945 by a group of countries called the Allies.

Europe and the Far East

The fighting mainly took place in Europe and the Far East, although many other parts of the world were also involved.

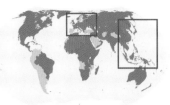

German refugee children in 1938

Children at war

Anti-Jewish laws forced Jewish children in Germany to escape to other countries, becoming refugees. Other children left their homes in cities to escape bombing.

D-day

The largest ever invasion from the sea took place on June 6, 1944. American, British, and Canadian troops crossed the English Channel and landed on the French coast to free France from German rule.

German U-boats (submarines) attacked Allied ships in the Atlantic.

In *1940*, Britain's Royal Air Force beat German planes in a battle in the sky.

NORWAY

SWEDEN

Leningrad 1941–1944

In June *1941*, the Axis powers almost knocked Russia out of the war with a huge attack.

Barbarossa

GREAT BRITAIN

Battle of Britain

ATLANTIC OCEAN

GERMANY

Spitfire

British and American planes regularly bombed German cities.

Blitzkrieg

Kursk, western Russia

POLAND

FRANCE

Germany took Poland by surprise with a "blitzkrieg," or lightning war.

German leader Hitler took over France in *1940*.

ITALY

Russia won the biggest ever tank battle against Germany at Kursk between July and August *1943*.

SPAIN

Monte Cassino, Italy, 1944

TURKEY

Jews in Germany were forced to wear yellow stars bearing the word "Jude"— German for Jew.

MEDITERRANEAN SEA

El Alamein, Egypt, 1942

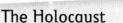

The Holocaust

The Nazis killed Jewish people just because they were Jewish. During the Holocaust, Jews were sent to camps to be killed. More than six million died.

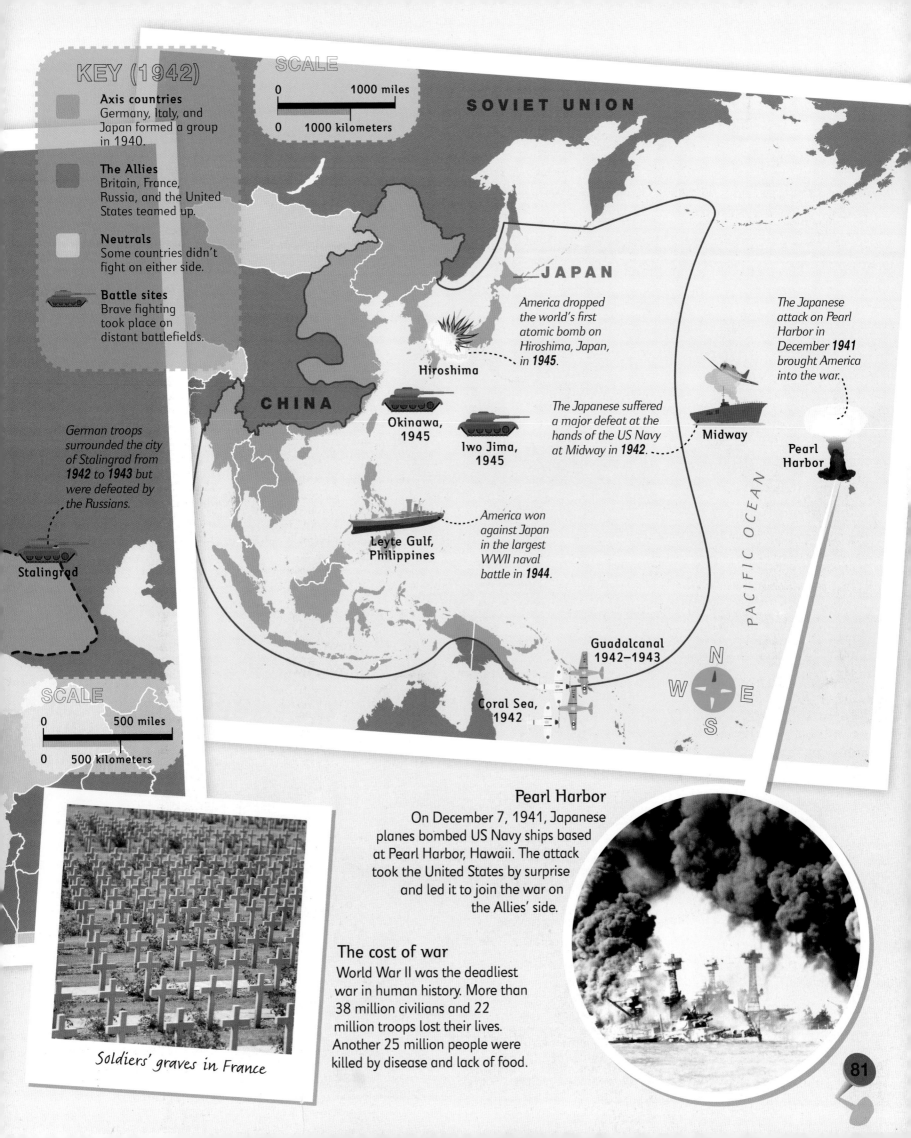

KEY (1942)

Axis countries
Germany, Italy, and Japan formed a group in 1940.

The Allies
Britain, France, Russia, and the United States teamed up.

Neutrals
Some countries didn't fight on either side.

Battle sites
Brave fighting took place on distant battlefields.

SCALE

0   1000 miles

0   1000 kilometers

JAPAN

*America dropped the world's first atomic bomb on Hiroshima, Japan, in **1945**.*

Hiroshima

*The Japanese attack on Pearl Harbor in December **1941** brought America into the war.*

CHINA

*The Japanese suffered a major defeat at the hands of the US Navy at Midway in **1942**.*

Midway

Pearl Harbor

Okinawa, 1945

Iwo Jima, 1945

*German troops surrounded the city of Stalingrad from **1942** to **1943** but were defeated by the Russians.*

*America won against Japan in the largest WWII naval battle in **1944**.*

Leyte Gulf, Philippines

Stalingrad

PACIFIC OCEAN

Guadalcanal 1942–1943

Coral Sea, 1942

N
W   E
S

SCALE

0   500 miles

0   500 kilometers

Pearl Harbor

On December 7, 1941, Japanese planes bombed US Navy ships based at Pearl Harbor, Hawaii. The attack took the United States by surprise and led it to join the war on the Allies' side.

The cost of war

World War II was the deadliest war in human history. More than 38 million civilians and 22 million troops lost their lives. Another 25 million people were killed by disease and lack of food.

Soldiers' graves in France

Independent world

In 1945, most of the world's nations were colonies, which meant they were ruled by other countries. Since then, most colonies have become independent. Some countries gained their freedom peacefully, while others had to fight for it. There are now 195 independent nations in the world.

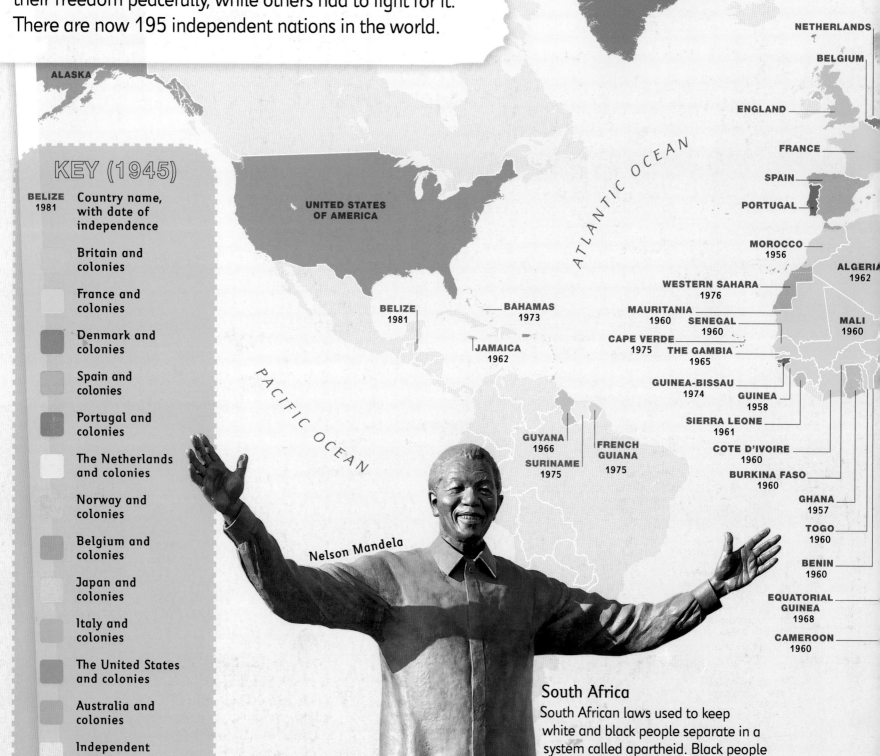

GREENLAND

ARCTIC O

NETHERLANDS

BELGIUM

ENGLAND

FRANCE

SPAIN

PORTUGAL

ALASKA

UNITED STATES OF AMERICA

ATLANTIC OCEAN

MOROCCO
1956

ALGERIA
1962

WESTERN SAHARA
1976

BELIZE
1981

BAHAMAS
1973

MAURITANIA
1960   SENEGAL
1960

MALI
1960

CAPE VERDE
1975   THE GAMBIA
1965

JAMAICA
1962

GUINEA-BISSAU
1974   GUINEA
1958

PACIFIC OCEAN

SIERRA LEONE
1961

COTE D'IVOIRE
1960

GUYANA
1966   FRENCH
GUIANA
1975

SURINAME
1975

BURKINA FASO
1960

GHANA
1957

TOGO
1960

Nelson Mandela

BENIN
1960

EQUATORIAL
GUINEA
1968

CAMEROON
1960

KEY (1945)

BELIZE
1981
Country name, with date of independence

Britain and colonies

France and colonies

Denmark and colonies

Spain and colonies

Portugal and colonies

The Netherlands and colonies

Norway and colonies

Belgium and colonies

Japan and colonies

Italy and colonies

The United States and colonies

Australia and colonies

Independent nations

South Africa

South African laws used to keep white and black people separate in a system called apartheid. Black people were treated as less important. Nelson Mandela led people against these laws. Apartheid finally ended in 1991.

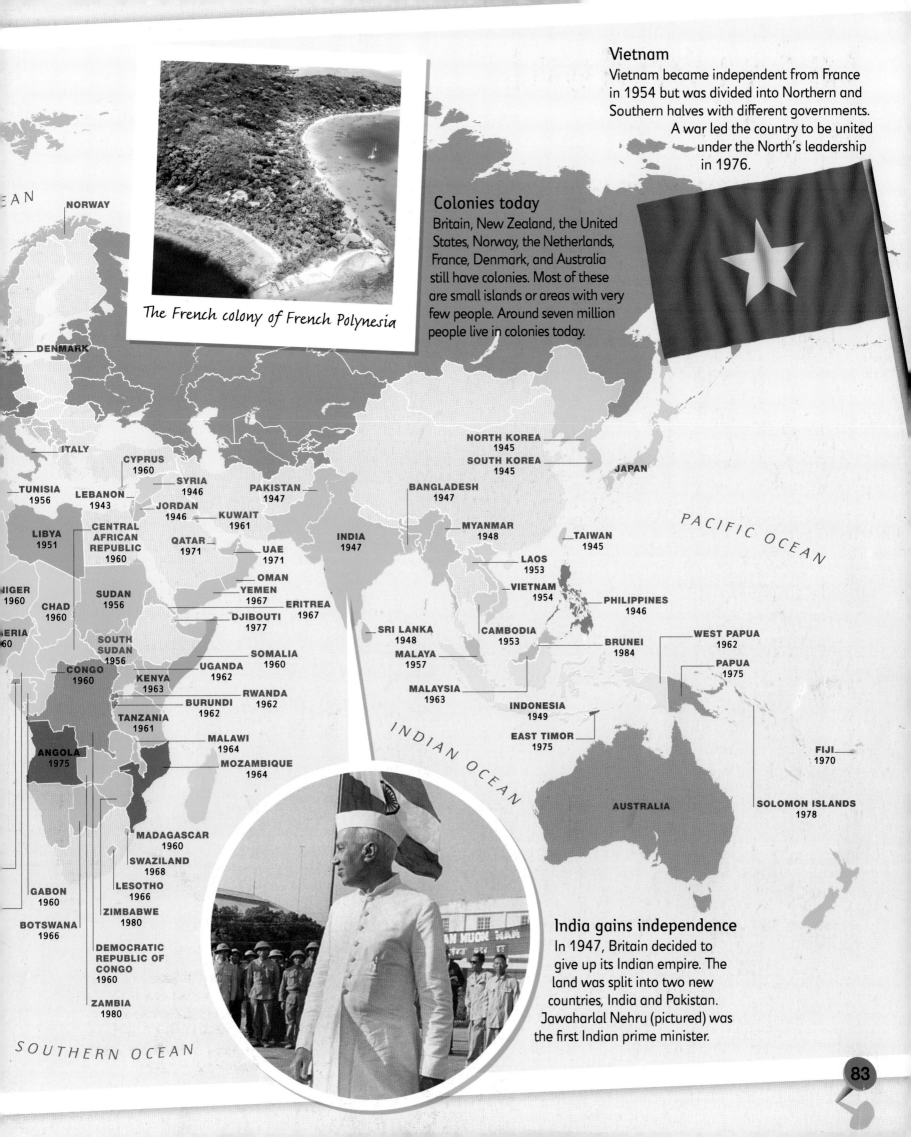

Vietnam
Vietnam became independent from France in 1954 but was divided into Northern and Southern halves with different governments. A war led the country to be united under the North's leadership in 1976.

The French colony of French Polynesia

Colonies today
Britain, New Zealand, the United States, Norway, the Netherlands, France, Denmark, and Australia still have colonies. Most of these are small islands or areas with very few people. Around seven million people live in colonies today.

NORWAY

DENMARK

OCEAN

ITALY

CYPRUS
1960

TUNISIA
1956

LEBANON
1943

SYRIA
1946

PAKISTAN
1947

BANGLADESH
1947

NORTH KOREA
1945

SOUTH KOREA
1945

JAPAN

JORDAN
1946

KUWAIT
1961

LIBYA
1951

CENTRAL
AFRICAN
REPUBLIC
1960

QATAR
1971

UAE
1971

INDIA
1947

MYANMAR
1948

TAIWAN
1945

PACIFIC OCEAN

OMAN

NIGER
1960

SUDAN
1956

YEMEN
1967

ERITREA
1967

LAOS
1953

VIETNAM
1954

CHAD
1960

DJIBOUTI
1977

PHILIPPINES
1946

NERIA
60

SOUTH
SUDAN
1956

SRI LANKA
1948

CAMBODIA
1953

WEST PAPUA
1962

CONGO
1960

UGANDA
1962

SOMALIA
1960

MALAYA
1957

BRUNEI
1984

PAPUA
1975

KENYA
1963

RWANDA
1962

MALAYSIA
1963

BURUNDI
1962

TANZANIA
1961

INDONESIA
1949

INDIAN OCEAN

ANGOLA
1975

MALAWI
1964

EAST TIMOR
1975

FIJI
1970

MOZAMBIQUE
1964

AUSTRALIA

SOLOMON ISLANDS
1978

MADAGASCAR
1960

SWAZILAND
1968

GABON
1960

LESOTHO
1966

ZIMBABWE
1980

BOTSWANA
1966

DEMOCRATIC
REPUBLIC OF
CONGO
1960

India gains independence
In 1947, Britain decided to give up its Indian empire. The land was split into two new countries, India and Pakistan. Jawaharlal Nehru (pictured) was the first Indian prime minister.

ZAMBIA
1980

SOUTHERN OCEAN

The Cold War

After World War II, two superpowers had different ideas about how to run the world. The communist USSR wanted everybody to be equal. The capitalist United States thought it was more important for people to be free. There was a Cold War, with America and the USSR taking opposite sides in struggles around the world between 1947 and 1991.

The Space Race
America and the USSR raced each other to get into space. The United States won when Neil Armstrong became the first person on the moon in 1969.

AMERICA SALUTES FIRST MEN ON THE MOON
ARMSTRONG   COLLINS   ALDRIN
APOLLO XI
JULY 1969

ARCTIC OCEAN

Radar stations along the Distance Early Warning (DEW) line would warn of a USSR bomber attack.

DEW line

The North Atlantic Treaty Organization (NATO) was an alliance led by the United States, set up in 1949.

NATO flag

NORTH AMERICA

KEY

NATO
Countries that were part of NATO— a capitalist group led by the United States.

Warsaw Pact
Communist countries that were part of the Warsaw Pact— an agreement with the USSR.

Non-NATO and Warsaw Pact
Countries that did not take part in the Cold War.

Conflicts
Foreign civil wars where the United States and the USSR supported different sides.

Uprisings
Revolts against governments in communist countries in Europe.

Spies
Places where spies operated.

Intercontinental ballistic missiles

Intercontinental missiles could carry nuclear warheads to destroy cities thousands of miles away.

Eisenhower and Khrushchev meet

In 1959 US President Eisenhower and the USSR's Secretary Khrushchev met to try to reduce the tension.

America and the USSR almost went to war when the USSR placed nuclear weapons in Cuba in 1962.

Cuban Missile Crisis

The United States funded rebels fighting the radical government of Nicaragua between 1978 and 1979.

Nicaraguan Revolution

PACIFIC OCEAN

ATLANTIC OCEAN

The hydrogen bomb
The first nuclear bomb was created during World War II. This atomic bomb was the most powerful weapon in history. During the Cold War, both sides developed an even more destructive nuclear bomb, called the hydrogen bomb.

First hydrogen bomb test, 1952

The divided city

After World War II, the German capital of Berlin was divided in two. The Western half was controlled by the United States, Britain, and France, while the USSR had the Eastern half. The city became the center of the Cold War.

Berlin blockade

From *1948* to *1949*, the USSR tried to block food from getting into West Berlin. Supplies were dropped in by planes.

Berlin wall

EAST BERLIN

WEST BERLIN

In *1961* East Berlin built a wall around the West to prevent Easterners from escaping there.

In *1955* the Warsaw Pact was set up as a military alliance between the USSR and six communist countries in Eastern Europe.

Warsaw Pact

The USSR's first intercontinental missile was launched in *1957*.

R-7 Semyorka

The USSR tested its first nuclear bomb in *1949*.

First Lightning

ASIA

In *1961*, Yuri Gagarin from the USSR became the first man in space.

Yuri Gagarin

China became a communist state in *1949* under Mao Zedong.

Chinese Civil War

Korean War

An attempt by communist North Korea to take over South Korea was stopped by American-led troops between *1950* and *1953*.

The Iron Curtain

EUROPE

The two sides of the Cold War faced each other across an "Iron Curtain" dividing Europe.

USSR and US soldiers helped different sides in Afghanistan between *1979* and *1989*.

Afghan War

Between *1964* and *1975*, US troops failed to help South Vietnam beat Communist North Vietnam.

Vietnam War

AFRICA

The United States and the USSR supported opposing sides in this war between *1975* and *2002*.

Angolan War

The end of the Cold War

In 1989, communist governments in Europe began to lose control. The Berlin Wall was pulled down in this year, and Germany was united in 1990. The USSR itself collapsed in 1991. The Cold War was over.

The fall of the Berlin Wall

Close enemies

The United States and the USSR faced each other across the Arctic Circle. At their closest, the countries were separated by only 2.4 miles (3.8 km).

The space age

The first human-made object left Earth in 1957—a tiny spacecraft called Sputnik. The Space Age had begun! A human flew in space for the first time in 1961, and people first walked on the moon in 1969. People have continued to explore space, finding out more and more about what exists beyond our world.

Landing on the surface of a comet

The Rosetta mission

On November 12, 2014, a spacecraft landed on a comet for the first time. Unfortunately, it landed in the shadow of a cliff and could not recharge its batteries, which were powered by the sun. After two days, its power ran out, and it went silent.

Man on the moon

On July 20, 1969, American Neil Armstrong became the first person to walk on the moon. Along with Buzz Aldrin, he spent about 150 minutes walking around and collecting rock samples.

In **1959**, the Luna 2 became the first spacecraft to reach the moon.

Luna 2

The first-ever satellite was launched into space by Russia on **October 4, 1957**. It was 23 in (58 cm) wide.

Sputnik 1

Jupiter

The sun

Venus

Mercury

Earth

Mars

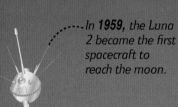

Mariner 10

The Mariner 10 traveled from Venus to Mercury between **1974** and **1975**.

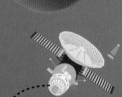

Venera 9

In **1975**, Venera 9 sent photographs of the surface of Venus to Earth.

Salyut 1

The first space station was launched into space by the Russians on **April 19, 1971**. It stayed there for 175 days.

Viking 2

The American Viking 2 spent 1,316 days on the surface of Mars, from **1976** to **1980**.

Pioneer 10

Pioneer 10 became the first spacecraft to leave the solar system, in **1983**.

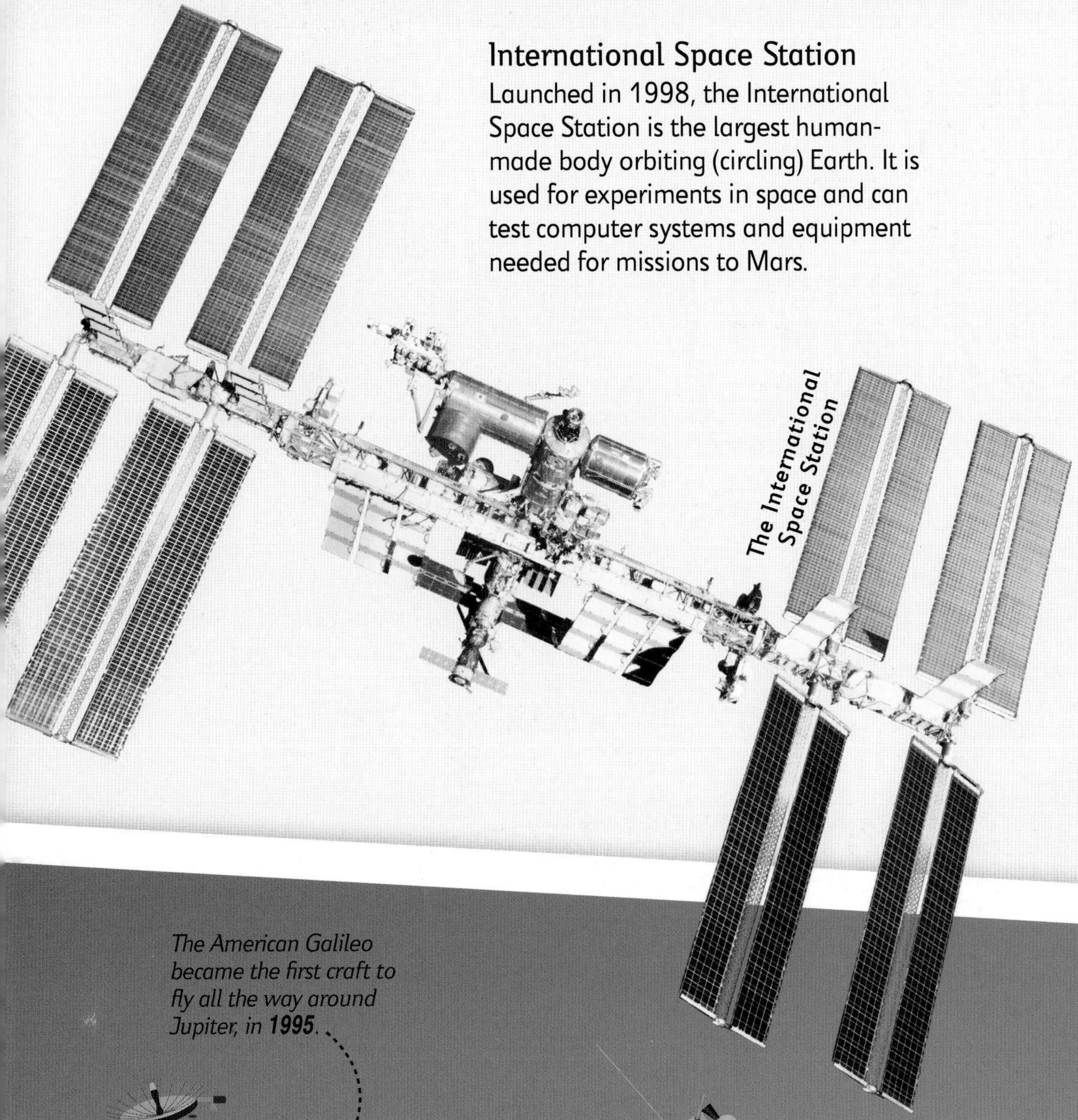

International Space Station

Launched in 1998, the International Space Station is the largest human-made body orbiting (circling) Earth. It is used for experiments in space and can test computer systems and equipment needed for missions to Mars.

The International Space Station

A satellite above Earth

Satellites

Sputnik I was the first satellite sent into space, in 1957. Today, satellites are used to transmit signals for TV programs and telephone calls. They also gather data about weather and locations for digital maps.

The American Galileo became the first craft to fly all the way around Jupiter, in 1995.

Galileo

Cassini was launched in 1997 and spent 13 years circling Saturn. It burned up in 2017.

Cassini

Saturn

Uranus

Neptune

Our solar system

Our solar system is made up of the eight planets that circle our sun. The image above shows them closer together than they really are.

The American Voyager 2 was the first space probe to visit outer planets Uranus and Neptune, in 1986 and 1989, respectively.

Voyager 2

The world today

Slightly fewer than eight billion people are alive in 2018, living in 195 countries. That number is expected to grow to 11.2 billion by the year 2100. China is the world's most populous nation, with around 8,800 Chinese babies born every day.

Uniting the world
The United Nations (UN), set up in 1945, is an organization that works to keep peace around the world. Almost every country today is a member of the UN.

World cities
In 2009, for the first time in history, more people lived in towns and cities than in the countryside. This trend is likely to continue as the world's population grows.

New York City

World's newest nation
New nations are still forming. The world's newest nation is South Sudan, which broke away from Sudan in 2011 after a long fight for independence.

GREENLAND (DENMARK)

ICELAND

ALASKA (UNITED STATES)

CANADA

NORTH AMERICA

UNITED STATES

HAWAII (UNITED STATES)

MEXICO
BELIZE
GUATEMALA
EL SALVADOR HONDURAS
NICARAGUA
COSTA RICA
PANAMA

CUBA
BAHAMAS
HAITI
DOMINICAN REPUBLIC
PUERTO RICO
ST KITTS & NEVIS
ANTIGUA & BARBUDA
DOMINICA
ST LUCIA
JAMAICA BARBADOS
GRENADA ST VINCENT & THE GRENADINES
TRINIDAD & TOBAGO

ALGERIA
MOROCCO
WESTERN SAHARA (DISPUTED)
MAURITANIA
SENEGAL
CAPE VERDE
THE GAMBIA
GUINEA-BISSAU
GUINEA
BURKINA FASO
SIERRA LEONE
LIBERIA
CÔTE D'IVOIRE
GHANA
TOGO
BENIN
CAMEROON
EQUATORIAL GUINEA
SÃO TOMÉ & PRÍNCIPE
GABON

MALI

VENEZUELA
COLOMBIA
GALÁPAGOS ISLANDS (ECUADOR)
ECUADOR
GUYANA
SURINAME
FRENCH GUIANA

SOUTH AMERICA

PERU
BOLIVIA
BRAZIL
PARAGUAY
CHILE
URUGUAY
ARGENTINA

PACIFIC OCEAN

ATLANTIC OCEAN

FALKLAND ISLANDS (UNITED KINGDOM)

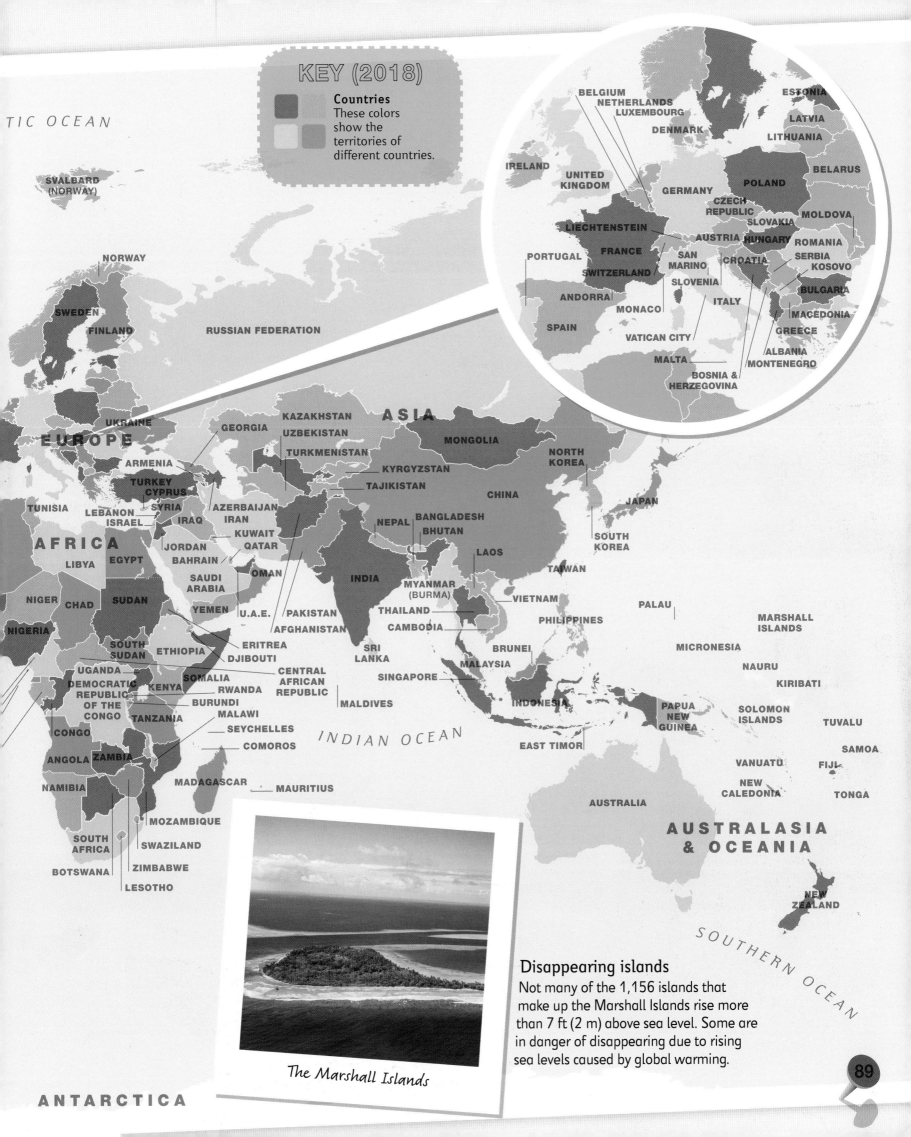

Disappearing islands

Not many of the 1,156 islands that make up the Marshall Islands rise more than 7 ft (2 m) above sea level. Some are in danger of disappearing due to rising sea levels caused by global warming.

The Marshall Islands

Atlas picture quiz

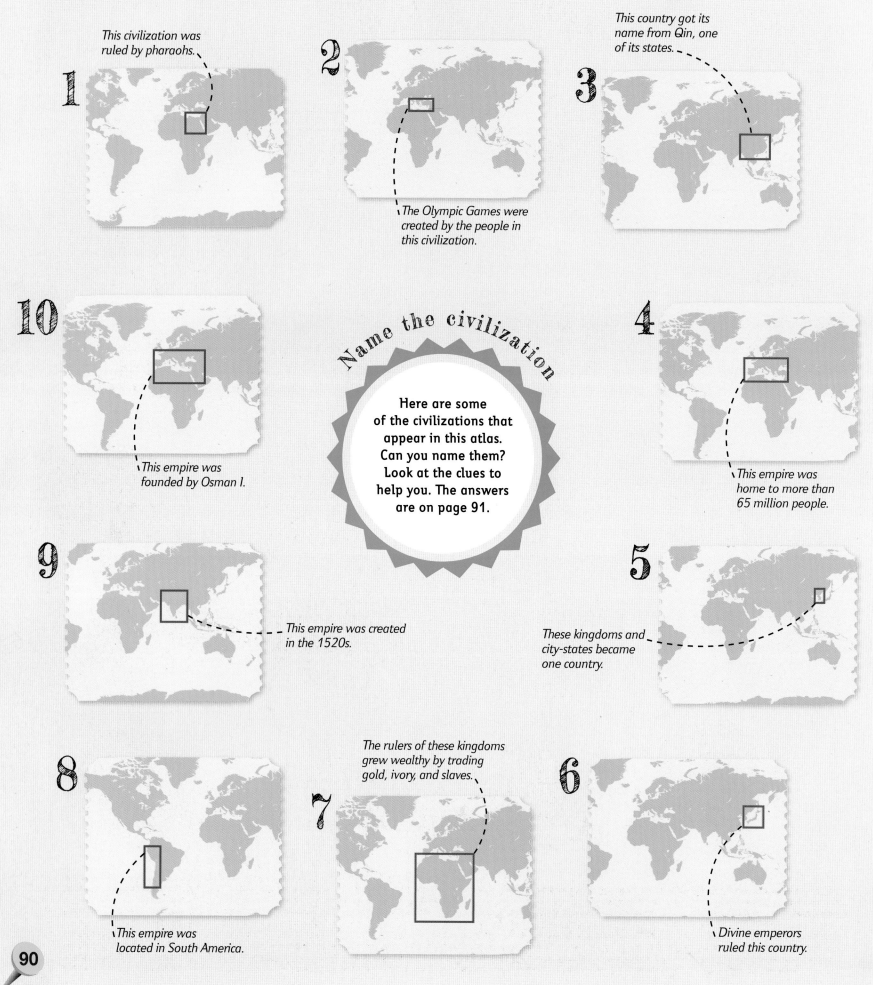

1 — This civilization was ruled by pharaohs.

2 — The Olympic Games were created by the people in this civilization.

3 — This country got its name from Qin, one of its states.

10 — This empire was founded by Osman I.

Name the civilization

Here are some of the civilizations that appear in this atlas. Can you name them? Look at the clues to help you. The answers are on page 91.

4 — This empire was home to more than 65 million people.

9 — This empire was created in the 1520s.

5 — These kingdoms and city-states became one country.

8 — This empire was located in South America.

7 — The rulers of these kingdoms grew wealthy by trading gold, ivory, and slaves.

6 — Divine emperors ruled this country.

All of the answers to these questions appear somewhere in this book. You can check if you are correct at the bottom of this page.

1. When did apes begin to walk upright?

2. Which country invented silk making?

3. What famous monument was built in Britain during the Stone Age?

4. What writing system was used by the ancient Egyptians?

5. Who were the most feared warriors in ancient Greece?

6. What was the First Emperor's tomb protected by?

7. What was the Colosseum used for?

8. Who were the first Europeans to reach America?

9. Which country has the world's oldest royal family?

10. Who are the native people of the Arctic?

11. What caused the spread of the Black Death?

12. In what year did Christopher Columbus reach the Americas?

13. What famous town in the Andes did the Incas build?

14. Why was the Taj Mahal built?

15. The famous sculpture of David was carved by which Renaissance artist?

16. How many African slaves were taken across the Atlantic?

17. On what date did America declare independence?

18. What did the 13th Amendment do?

19. What did Alexander Graham Bell invent?

20. During World War II, what were Jewish people forced to wear?

21. Who led the movement against apartheid in South Africa?

22. During the Cold War, what nuclear weapon did the US develop?

23. Who was the first person to walk on the moon?

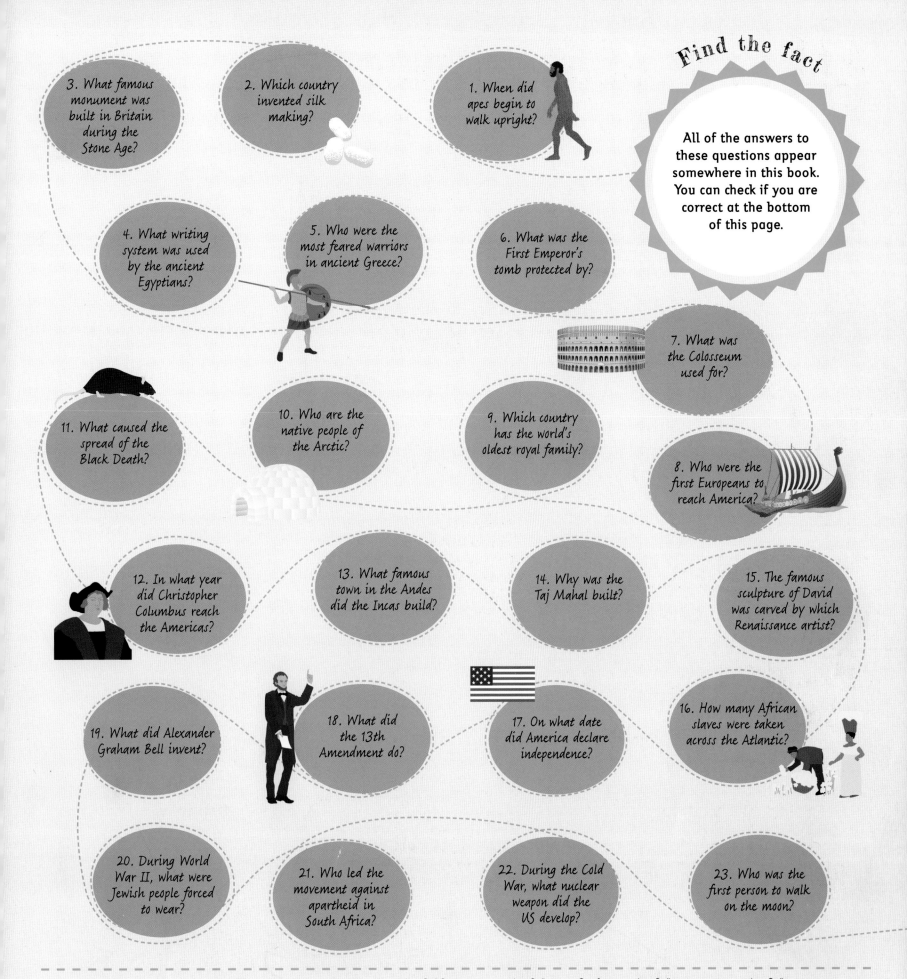

Answers: Page 8–9 The ancient world: 1. Jericho, 2. Valley of the Kings, 3. A wooden horse, 4. Nile, 5. Vercingetorix, 6. Mesopotamia, 7. The Xiongnu, 8. Mount Vesuvius. **Page 26–27 The Middle Ages:** 1. Buddhism, 2. Sahara, 3. Japan, 4. North America, 5. 1337, 6. The Mongols, 7. North America, 8. Black Death. **Page 42–43 The age of discovery:** 1. Inca Empire, 2. Emperor Shah Jahan, 3. Constantinople, 4. São Gabriel, 5. El Castillo, 6. India, 7. Pacal of Palenque, 8. Bastille. **Page 58 – 59 The age of industry:** 1. Yorktown, 2. James Hargreaves, 3. July 4, 1776, 4. Abraham Lincoln, 5. Tea, 6. Cornwall, 7. Bastille. **Page 70–71 The modern world:** 1. Ottoman Empire, 2. 1926, 3. 1939, 4. US, 5. Italy, 6. 1989, 7. South Sudan. **Page 90 Name the civilization:** 1. Egyptian (pages 16–17), 2. Greek (pages 18–19), 3. Chinese (pages 20–21), 4. Roman (pages 22–23), 5. Korean (pages 32–33), 6. Japanese (pages 32–33), 7. African (pages 36–37), 8. Inca (pages 46–47), 9. Mughal (pages 50–51), 10. Ottoman (pages 52–53). **Page 91 Find the fact:** 1. Around six million years ago (page 6), 2. China (page 11), 3. Stonehenge (page 12), 4. Hieroglyphs (page 16), 5. The Spartans (page 19), 6. A terra-cotta army (page 20), 7. To hold gladiator fights and other sports (page 23), 8. The Vikings (page 30), 9. Japan (page 33), 10. The Inuit (page 34), 11. Rat fleas (page 41), 12. 1492 (page 45), 13. Machu Picchu (page 47), 14. The Mughal emperor, Shah Jahan, built it in memory of his favorite wife (page 51), 15. Michelangelo (page 55), 16. 12 million (page 56), 17. July 4, 1776 (page 61), 18. It abolished slavery in the United States (page 67), 19. The first telephone (page 75), 20. A yellow star with the word "Jude" written on it (page 80), 21. Nelson Mandela (page 82), 22. The hydrogen bomb (page 84), 23. Neil Armstrong (page 86).

Glossary

agriculture
Growing crops and raising livestock for food

ally
Country that supports another country and might agree to trade deals or to fight alongside it in a war

ancient
Very old

army
Organized group of soldiers

artifact
Human-made object, generally of historic or cultural interest, such as a painting or a vase

astronaut
Someone who is trained to travel and work in a spacecraft

BCE
Before Common Era, or all the years before year 1

beliefs
Set of views that people hold about the world, life, and the afterlife

Buddhist
Member of a religion called Buddhism, which follows the teachings of the Buddha, who lived in India about 2,500 years ago

capitalism
Political or economic system where individuals own property and companies, instead of the government owning them

CE
Common Era, or all the years after year 1

Christian
Someone who follows the religious teachings of Jesus Christ, who lived in the Middle East 2,000 years ago

civilization
Society where people have built a complex city or country

colony
Area of land or island belonging to a different country

conquer
Act of one country taking over another country

culture
Way of life and beliefs of the people of a region or country

democracy
System of government where people outside the government have a say in how the country is run, usually by voting

dictator
Ruler with total power

emperor
Ruler of an empire

empire
Large area with different peoples, ruled by a king/queen or emperor/emperess

government
Group of people who run a country

Hindu
Member of the Indian religion Hinduism. Hindus worship many gods and believe that when people die they are born again

holy
Something or somewhere sacred to a religion

independence
Freedom from outside control, such as when a country or area is no longer ruled by another country

Jew
Follower of the religion Judaism. Jews worship one God and their holy books are the Hebrew Bible (Old Testament) and the Talmud

Muslim
Someone whose religion is Islam. Muslims believe in one God, and they follow the teachings of the Prophet Muhammad

native
Person linked to a place by birth, or who is descended from the original inhabitants of an area

Nazi
Member, or follower, of the Nazi Party (National Socialists) in Germany, led by Adolf Hitler

peasant
A poor person whose way of life is dependent on farming

persecution
Bad treatment of people because of their beliefs

Renaissance
A focus on art and learning in Europe that began in the 15th century, linked to a renewed interest in the ancient cultures of Greece and Rome

revolution
Sudden change that happens when a government or ruling power is overthrown, often quickly and by force

slave
Person who is forced to work for or serve another person or family. Slaves are considered the property of their owners and forced to obey them

society
Organized group of people with a shared culture

spy
Person who gathers information in secret. In war, each side uses spies to find out the other's secrets

technology
Using scientific knowledge to create machinery and devices, such as computers

territory
Area of land that belongs to a particular country or state

trade route
Route traveled by merchants carrying goods from one country to another

traditional
When something has been done in the same way for a long time

tribe
Group of people who share the same culture and history. It usually refers to people who live together in traditional communities, far from cities and towns

Index

Credits

Dorling Kindersley would like to thank the following people for their assistance in the preparation of this book: Caroline Hunt for proofreading and Helen Peters for the index.

Picture Credits:
The publisher would also like to thank the following for their kind permission to reproduce their photographs:

(Key: a-above; b-below/bottom; c-center; f-far; l-left; r-right; t-top)

6 Dorling Kindersley: Dave King/National Museum of Wales (bl). Science Photo Library: S. ENTRESSANGLE/E. DAYNES (tr). **7 Alamy Stock Photo**: Image Gap (bc). Neanderthal Museum: (tl). **10 Alamy Stock Photo**: ping han (br). Dreamstime.com: Blossfeldia (clb). **10-11 Dorling Kindersley**: Gary Ombler/The Combined Military Services Museum (CMSM) (c). **11 Alamy Stock Photo**: INTERFOTO (clb). **Dreamstime.com**: Christian Delbert/Babar760 (br); Carlos1967 (cla); Jeanne Coppens /Moramora (cra); Keith Wheatley/Kwheatley (c). **Getty Images**: De Agostini Picture Library (tc). iStockphoto.com: Aleksandr_Vorobev (crb). **12 Alamy Stock Photo**: PRISMA ARCHIVO (clb). **13 Alamy Stock Photo**: Robert Hoetink (br). **Getty Images**: DEA PICTURE LIBRARY (tc); DEA/G. DAGLI ORTI (tr). **14 Alamy Stock Photo**: MuseoPics - Paul Williams (bl). **Dorling Kindersley**: Gary Ombler/The University of Aberdeen (cr). **15 Alamy Stock Photo**: JTB MEDIA CREATION, Inc. (cl); robertharding (tr). **16 Dreamstime**.com: Blossfeldia (br); Diego Elorza/ Diegophoto (cla). **17 Dorling Kindersley**: Alistair Duncan/Cairo Museum (br); Gary Ombler/The University of Aberdeen (tr). **18 Alamy Stock Photo**: Science History Images (br). **Dreamstime.com**: Gigavisual (clb). **19 Dreamstime.com**: Sofia Katsikadi/Sofiakat17 (tl). **20 Alamy Stock Photo**: World History Archive (cl). **Dreamstime.com**: Steve Allen/Mrallen (bl). **21 Dorling Kindersley**: Gary Ombler / University of Pennsylvania Museum of Archaeology and Anthropology (cr/ coins. **Dreamstime.com**: Silvershot55 (tr). **22 Alamy Stock Photo**: A. Astes (bc); Adam Eastland (c). **24 123RF.com**: taigi (cl). **Dorling Kindersley**: Ray Moller/Powell-Cotton Museum, Kent. (br). **Dreamstime.com**: Ahmad Faizal Yahya/Afby71 (tr). **Getty Images**: Godong (tl). **25 Alamy Stock Photo**: Art Directors & TRIP (tl). **Dreamstime.com**: Woraphon Banchobdi/Pat138241 (bc). **iStockphoto.com**: aluxum (tr). **28 Dorling Kindersley**: Dave King/ University Museum of Archaeology and Anthropology, Cambridge (tr). **Getty Images**: DEA / G. DAGLI ORTI (c). **29 Alamy Stock Photo**: Ian Bottle (c). **Dorling Kindersley**: Dave King/Durham University Oriental Museum (cra); Gary Ombler/Vikings of Middle England (ca/shield & axe). **Getty Images**: GraphicaArtis (clb). **30 Alamy Stock Photo**: Rami Aapasuo (tr). **30-31 Dreamstime.com**: Lucian Milasan/Miluxian (bc). **31 Dorling Kindersley**: Peter Anderson/Universitets Oldsaksamling, Oslo (br/helmet); Gary Ombler/Vikings of Middle England (tr); Gary Ombler/Canterbury City Council, Museums and Galleries (tr/ring); Dave King/ Museum of London (br/axe). **Getty Images**: Print

Collector (cl). **32 Alamy Stock Photo**: JeongHyeon Noh (tl); SuperStock (cl). **33 Alamy Stock Photo**: ART Collection (cl). **Dreamstime.com**: Srlee2 (br). **34 Getty Images**: Apic/RETIRED (tl); MPI/Stringer (c). **35 Alamy Stock Photo**: Granger Historical Picture Archive (bc). **36 Alamy Stock Photo**: Gavin Hellier (bc); Ian Nellist (cla). **37 Alamy Stock Photo**: Chris Howes/Wild Places Photography (c). **Getty Images**: DEA/W. BUSS (t); Historical Picture Archive (cr). **38 Alamy Stock Photo**: Granger Historical Picture Archive (bc); North Wind Picture Archives (cl); imageBROKER (cb). **Dorling Kindersley**: Gary Ombler/Canterbury City Council, Museums and Galleries (bl). **39 Dorling Kindersley**: Dave King / Durham University Oriental Museum (tc). **40 Dreamstime.com**: Leonid Andronov (tr); Tupungato (cl). **iStockphoto.com**: ManuWe (bl). **41 Alamy Stock Photo**: PRISMA ARCHIVO (tr). **Getty Images**: Hulton Archive/Stringer (br). **44 Alamy Stock Photo**: Hilary Morgan (cra); PAINTING (cb). **Dorling Kindersley**: Eric Isselee/isselee (clb). **Dreamstime.com**: Neophuket (bc). **45 Alamy Stock Photo**: Bruce yuanyue Bi (tc); GL Archive (br). **Dreamstime.com**: Mik3812345 (ca). **46 Dreamstime.com**: Steve Estvanik (tr). **47 Alamy Stock Photo**: World History Archive (tl). **Dorling Kindersley**: Hoa Luc (tr); Hoa Luc (cl). **48 Alamy Stock Photo**: Hirarchivum Press (bl). **49 123RF.com**: Sergey Kolesnikov (br/clove). **Alamy Stock Photo**: Lanmas (tr). **Dreamstime.com**: Albertocc311 (br/black pepper). **50 Alamy Stock Photo**: IndiaPicture (tl). **51 Alamy Stock Photo**: Dinodia Photos (br). Dreamstime.com: Neophuket (tl). **52 Getty Images**: Heritage Images (br). **53 Alamy Stock Photo**: MARKA (tr). **54 Alamy Stock Photo**: North Wind Picture Archives (cl). **Getty Images**: De Agostini/G. Cigolini/Veneranda Biblioteca Ambrosiana (bl). **55 123RF.com**: flik47 (tr); Lomet (crb). **56 Getty Images**: Henry Guttmann/Stringer (tl); Hulton Archive/ Stringer (cl). **57 Alamy Stock Photo**: Pictorial Press Ltd (br). **60 Alamy Stock Photo**: World History Archive (crb). **Getty Images**: Hulton Archive/Stringer (ca). **60-61 Alamy Stock Photo**: Arco Images GmbH (c/napolean). **61 Dorling Kindersley**: Dave King/The Science Museum, London (cra); Gary Ombler/National Railway Museum, York/Science Museum Group (c); Clive Streeter/ The Science Museum, London (clb). **62 123RF.com**: Rolando Da Jose/annika09 (br). **63 Dreamstime.com**: Lenise Zerafa/Esinel (tl); Georgios Kollidas (clb). **64 Getty Images**: Science & Society Picture Library (cla). SuperStock: Iberfoto (tc). **65 Dorling Kindersley**: Dave King/The Science Museum, London (tr). **iStockphoto. com**: whitemay (br). **66 Alamy Stock Photo**: US National Archives (tr). **67 Getty Images**: Corbis Historical (br). **68 Alamy Stock Photo**: World History Archive (cl). **69 Dreamstime.com**: Chrisp543 (bl). **Getty Images**: Pascal Sebah/Stringer (tl). **72 123RF.com**: alessandro0770 (bl). **Dorling Kindersley**: Gary Ombler/John Pearce (tc). **Dreamstime.com**: Anusorn62 (cb). **73 Dorling Kindersley**: Ellen Howdon/Glasgow Museums/Glasgow City Council (Museums) (tl); Gary Ombler/Royal Museum of the Armed Forces and of Military History, Brussels,

Belgium (cb). **Dreamstime.com**: Gail Benson/ Digitaldaisyza (bl); Oleksii Popov/Simfalex (tr). **74 Alamy Stock Photo**: ClassicStock (cl). **Getty Images**: Hoberman Collection (bl). **75 Dorling Kindersley**: Clive Streeter/ The Science Museum, London (br). **76 Alamy Stock Photo**: Universal Images Group North America LLC (cb). **Getty Images**: Henry Guttmann (cl). **77 Getty Images**: Hulton Deutsch (tr); Hulton Archive/Stringer (cr). **78 Getty Images**: Hulton Archive/Stringer (br). **79 Getty Images**: Bettmann (tr); Central Press/Stringer (bl). **80 Alamy Stock Photo**: World History Archive (bl). **Dorling Kindersley**: Andy Crawford/Imperial War Museum, London/By kind permission of The Trustees of the Imperial War Museum, London (bc). **Getty Images**: Fred Morley/Stringer (cl). **81 Getty Images**: Photo 12 (br). **83 Dreamstime.com**: Hel080808 (tc). **Getty Images**: Howard Sochurek (bc). **84 Getty Images**: Blank Archives (tr); Science & Society Picture Library (br). **85 Alamy Stock Photo**: Agencja Fotograficzna Caro (br). **86 Dorling Kindersley**: NASA (cl). NASA: ESA (tr). **87 Dreamstime.com**: Andrey Armyagov (tr). NASA: (tl). **88 123RF.com**: Peter Etchells / peteretchells (br). **Dreamstime.com**: Songquan Deng (bl). **Getty Images**: Image Source / United Nations (cl). **89 Alamy Stock Photo**: Greg Vaughn (bc)

All other images © Dorling Kindersley

For further information see: www.**dkimages**.com